Goal Setting and

Daily Habits

2-in-1 Bundle

How to Master Goal Setting,
Develop Winning Habits and
Elevate Yourself to the Top

ROMNEY NELSON

*This book is dedicated to all of you that want to live life to the **MAX** and Take Action Daily!*

TABLE OF CONTENTS

Goal Setting and Daily Habits

INTRODUCTION

Even with the best intentions, we do not always achieve what we set out to do in life. Maybe you are looking to improve your health by eating right and exercising, but your gym attendance starts to slip by the end of the first month. Perhaps you would like to improve your relationships, but you never follow through on your plans to meet up with people and keep those connections strong. You would love to travel, but you unconsciously find any excuse to avoid booking the trip. You want to do better at work and get that promotion you've had your eye on, but you just aren't sure where to start. After all of this difficulty, setting and achieving goals may even feel like an impossibility. You have likely tried to follow goal setting guides before, but you feel as though you don't have the time or energy to devote to them. If you are part of the typical 9 to 5, 40-hour workweek, you likely come home exhausted, stuck in a vicious cycle of thinking about everything you're going to start on the weekend and never quite have the energy to get it done. You want to succeed, but you feel as though it's just not in the cards for you. At this point, you may be asking yourself, where would I even begin when it comes to goal setting? How can I find the time to achieve my goals? Is there any way for me to establish the habits that will allow me to achieve more and improve my health, relationships, and wealth?

Failing to meet the goals you set for yourself can cause you to feel stuck as if you have hit a speed bump in life and you can't seem to get past it. But you still have the ability to achieve your goals, and with the right tools, you will be clearing the speed bump in no time, well on your way to success.

In this book, I will show you a simple and effective 7-step process that anyone can implement into even the busiest of schedules to achieve more than you ever thought possible. There are two brand new and exclusive systems outlined in this book. Firstly, you will be introduced to a method known as **DR. ACTION™**, and it will allow you to establish and even surpass goals to benefit your health, wealth, self, and happiness. The second process is called **'The Goal Loop'**, and it will guide you through the cyclical process of establishing goals, developing supportive habits and then celebrating your achievements.

This book will give you clear and actionable steps that help you to:

- Understand the psychology behind goal setting and implement it to your benefit
- Master goal setting and plan your path to success
- Learn about the power of micro-actions and how you can take over 1,000 micro-actions each year to achieve your dream goals
- Create and utilize supportive daily habits that will guarantee success
- Add an extra three months a year to your schedule so that you can improve your mental and physical health, increase your knowledge and achieve your goals faster than you ever thought to be possible.
- Confront and overcome tendencies towards procrastination and feelings of insecurity, fear, and limiting beliefs that are holding you back.

- Increase self-confidence, boost your energy levels and finally know the path to achieve your goals.

If all of this sounds like a mere fantasy, it is time to change your mindset and ditch feelings of uncertainty and doubt. Once you believe that you can do it, the path ahead becomes clear.

My name is Romney Nelson, and I have dedicated the last 20 years of my life to improving the success of others by developing beneficial systems and support structures that allow them to establish short-term and long-term goals and achieve massive success. I believe I can help you to do the same if you follow the steps outlined in Magnetic Goals.

To delve further into my background, I am a Motivational Speaker, Author, High-Performance Coach, National Sporting Representative Entrepreneur and an Executive Coach & Mentor. I want to share everything that I have learned from these positions of coaching to help you win the game of life and take you to the next level of success.

With some clarity, discipline, and simple daily actions, you can develop the momentum in mere weeks that will carry you onward to achieving lifelong goals. I want you to know exactly what your version of success looks like so that you can start developing a plan of action to accomplish your goals, whatever they may be. Doing so is only a matter of following the 7-step plan.

The Benefits of the 7-Step Plan

Following the 7-step plan as outlined in *Magnetic Goals* will show you how to develop your goals in as little as an hour. The early investment of just one hour will yield life-changing results in the form of positive daily habits that support your confidence and the development of a growth mindset. Changing your foundational beliefs from self-critical to a more positive, ambitious outlook will help you better understand just what prevents people from following through on their goals and what you can do to avoid the same fate. Like a magnet, you will learn how to attract positive opportunities into your life as you develop an optimistic mindset that turns setbacks and challenges into learning opportunities for personal growth. Changing your point of view will completely change your life.

My clients have transformed their lives just by

following the 7-step plan and incorporating its tenets into their daily lives. You too can achieve everything you set out to do, but first, you must commit yourself to the change. This means developing a focused mindset and believing in yourself. If growing your wealth, improving your relationships, and supporting your physical and mental health is important to you, the 7-step plan will ensure nothing stands in your way.

The success that you have always sought, even for goals that may seem like only a pleasant daydream, is achievable. The steps to make it happen are available. The time to make it happen is right now. Commit yourself to change by following the 7-step plan for three months, just 90 days, and see real, measurable results. As long as you have the reason and the drive to make it happen, and you are at the point in your life where you are ready to devote yourself to your passions, the 7-step plan will help you accomplish everything you set out to do.

From the age of 40, you may only have 600 more months on earth to make the change should you live to 90. There is no time to delay, and if you are truly passionate about achieving your goals, you will stop leaving life on cruise control and hit the gas pedal now. Start today, not tomorrow. Remember, when you look back on your life you won't regret the things you did try, but the things you never attempted. Taking action and utilize your time to the fullest is the most important thing you can do in this moment.

Your new growth mindset begins by following the steps outlined in *Magnetic Goals*. Don't allow a single day to go to waste from this point forward, and don't let your goals slip away. This book contains the blueprints and advice you need to become successful. You are too important to let this opportunity pass you by. It is time to start the path to your new life and begin taking action.

Step 1

The Belief to Make It Happen

In order to achieve success, you must believe that it is possible. Allowing yourself to be weighed down by thoughts of hopelessness and self-doubt will only ever weaken your attempts to improve your life. Knowing that you are capable of reaching your goals and surpassing expectations, however, can give you the boost that you need to commit to your new journey. The first step on the path to success is changing your ingrained beliefs, mindset, developing supporting structures and the systems for your journey. Developing the right mindset can be one of the hardest steps; after all, you may have spent your whole life letting feelings of inadequacy accumulate without attempting to challenge them. As a result, it can be hard to know what exactly you want to accomplish and how to set goals to pursue those dreams, as you don't yet believe that supposedly lofty goals are within your grasp. Putting in the work to alter your outlook and discovering your definition of success is a powerful first step that will snowball into much more significant changes as you proceed through the 7-step method. Stop believing you can't and start accepting that you can and will win.

Developing the Success Mindset

What is the success mindset? As the name implies, it is an outlook on life that aids you in achieving what you set out to do. A good mindset can help you overcome fears of failure and minimize feelings of uncertainty that keep you from getting things done. To even begin to achieve your goals, you have to believe that they are possible. Failing to do so can cause you to ignore opportunities and give up after minor failures. But if you engage in the success mindset, you will stop seeing temporary setbacks as anything other than learning experiences. You will begin to look for possible opportunities for growth and advancement in every part of life, and you will have the confidence to accept those opportunities when they occur. Your mindset should be empowering and encouraging, strong enough to withstand any setback and flexible enough to seek new opportunities. Once you start looking at the world through this lens, obstacles on the path to achieving your goals will begin to vanish in front of your very eyes.

The success mindset also shares similarities with the growth mindset. Both help you to achieve your goals, and both encourage hard work instead of relying on chance and circumstance. Carol Dweck, the author of 'Mindset', summarizes this well by explaining that "individuals who believe their talents can be developed (through hard work, good strategies, and input from others) have a growth mindset. They tend to achieve more than those with a fixed mindset (those who believe their talents are innate gifts)". Adopting the growth mindset is much more beneficial for accomplishing your goals, especially if you have found difficulty in doing so in the past. You can change, learn, and grow from your past so long as you apply yourself, and your hard work will pay off in the form of success.

The first step in this process is figuring out exactly what success means to you. Being able to envision your goals allows you to make concrete, specific plans that take you closer and closer to achieving them. Without knowing where you are going, you could be wandering aimlessly along the path of life for months or even years, making no progress towards your goals. This wastes precious time, which is one of the most valuable things we have on this earth and should never be carelessly thrown away. Figuring out your definition of success can take a little bit of soul searching, but ultimately, it is merely a matter of answering a few questions.

Defining Success

If I were to ask you what you really wanted to achieve in life, what would you say? What would it look like to you? Does financial security and freedom matter the most to you? Are you more concerned with having and taking care of a family? Are you interested in pursuing fame and glory, getting the recognition you have been fighting for, or do you care more about deep interpersonal connections and strong relationships? None of these goals are inherently good or bad, but some may resonate with you more so than others. Identifying which are most important to you can help you focus your efforts and make decisions that correlate with your desired outcome.

On the other hand, is it fulfilling to have just one of these goals without some aspects of the others? Put aside your preconceived notions of what is realistic for a moment and just think about what it would feel like to accomplish each of these goals. Would you be happy being rich and famous if it meant you had no one to really talk to? Conversely, could you really take good care of your family if you didn't have the financial means to keep them happy and healthy? Contrary to popular belief, it is possible to achieve these seemingly disparate goals together. Being successful in your career does not have to mean putting the rest of your life on hold, and caring genuinely about those around you does not mean you have to neglect your work either. To define your personal version of success, consider what your ideal life would look like and what combination of goals would be part of it. Real success should be the realization of your goals across a cross-section of health, wealth, self, and happiness, in whatever form that means for you. Pursuing these key pillars of a successful life will help you accomplish your goals in a balanced, healthy manner.

Taking Charge

Knowing what your goals are also involves understanding that, at the end of the day, you and you alone are responsible for your success. You cannot rely on pure chance or the charity of others to get where you need to go if you are serious about making a change. You may indeed have had difficult or painful life experiences and roadblocks to achieving success that others may not have experienced. Still, it doesn't mean you cannot move past these setbacks and achieve just as much as, if not more than anyone else. It is going to take dedication, unwavering commitment and effort, but if you do not put in the work, no one else is going to put it in for you. The support of friends and family is a powerful motivator, but at the end of the day, the results of your life are in your own hands. Your success is your personal responsibility – nobody else's.

Unlocking Your Limiting Beliefs

We all have insecurities and uncertainties that may come to light whenever we most need confidence. When these feelings prevent you from acting or keep you from living up to your full potential, they are known as limiting beliefs. Limiting beliefs can be targeted internally or externally. Internal beliefs are those you hold about yourself. These are often thoughts of self-consciousness, self-doubt, and negativity towards your own abilities. They may even cause you to feel unworthy of success, holding you back from pursuing it further. External beliefs are about the people around you and the world at large. Thinking everyone is out to get you and that the world will never allow you to succeed can prevent you from even trying in the first place. Both internal and external negativity can keep you stagnant in life.

Limiting beliefs are like locks that separate you from your potential successes. They keep you right where you are and make it seem impossible for you to access happiness and prosperity. These locks have kept your forward momentum imprisoned for far too long. In order to surpass them, you need a "key" – the optimistic outlook and self-confidence that will allow you to unlock the limiting beliefs and leave them in the dust as you move forward. This book will help you do that.

Establishing Absolute Clarity on What You Really Want

You cannot accomplish your goals if you do not have a firm grasp on what exactly they are. But answering this question can be more complicated than it seems. As a kid, you were likely asked what you wanted to be when you grow up, and it probably took you little time to come up with an answer like an astronaut, actor, or athlete. As you got older, you may have started seeing these jobs as unrealistic or outside of your skillset, and set them aside even if they still appealed to you. I am not merely suggesting that you pursue that astronaut job; you have had many years to develop interests and experience, and your dream job likely lies elsewhere now. Instead, consider how easy it was to know what you wanted and firmly believe you were capable of getting it. You did not waste time convincing yourself you would never achieve your goals, and as a result, you knew exactly what those goals were. Setting goals as an adult is, in a sense, an attempt to get back to that confident, assured idea of your future life that you once held. Consider what matters to you and what it would mean to you to achieve it. Maybe your dream job really hasn't changed over the years, or perhaps you discovered something entirely new that you would like to pursue. Maybe your goals don't involve a particular job at all, but rather focus on the development of your personal happiness and relationships with those around you. Either way, do not worry about being cautious or practical in your plans. Just consider what the optimal outcome is for you. If you take the time to set your goals and follow the 7-step plan, any goal you set is within your grasp.

The critical factor in setting goals at this stage in your life is clarity. Any idea you have for your future should be well-defined, and you should know exactly what outcome you are looking to achieve. Any overly general desire, like "making more money," should instead be clarified by isolating a specific job or pathway that will allow you to do so. Experts in the field like Brian Tracy, International Best-Selling Author and Speaker suggests that a "lack of clarity is probably more responsible for frustration and underachievement than any other single factor". Not knowing where you are going or having any idea of how to get there is a little like starting a road trip without a map or even a destination. It is a recipe for getting lost and wasting your time which could be entirely avoided by proper planning.

This also means determining what timeframe your goals should be accomplished in, as well as what order to achieve them. If, for example, one of your goals is to become a doctor, you cannot complete that goal until you have first completed schooling, and you should aim to complete your education in a reasonable amount of time for the best results. Failing to set timeframes and order your goals properly can hold you back and keep you treading water instead of providing you with a sense of urgency that encourages you to keep moving forward.

The Importance of Setting Goals

Setting firm, well-defined goals is the best way to ensure you maintain clarity in your pursuit of success. You can accomplish this by working backward from what you want to achieve. You wouldn't get on a plane without knowing where you want to end up, and similarly, you can't make progress in your life without knowing where you are trying to go. Goals provide you with a destination you can work backward from to plot out a strategy for achieving nearly anything by breaking it down into manageable chunks. Knowing your end result lets you develop the activities and habits that are critical to achieving what you want.

To set your goals, it may help to picture a sort of board game. At one end, there is an overarching goal that represents the final results of your work. In between, you need to 'roll the dice' and perhaps move one step forward but risk moving five steps backwards. Once you have finally reached this goal, you have effectively won the game, but there are many steps in between victory and the starting line. You effectively need to work backward, defining the next closest step in the series of events that will take you to the end of the board. Each goal should be in the service of the one after it so that every step you take is getting you closer to your final results. The most effective goals, therefore, are those that fall in line with your idea of the definition of success.

Knowing What Success Really Means to You

Defining success, like establishing your goals, is not always an easy process. Our lives are full of variety and many disparate elements coming together to form a cohesive whole. Trying to decide what the finished product of all aspects of your life should be, or pinning down the ideal versions of each element of your life, can be challenging. Work, family, and the inner self all play a role in determining exactly what success means. As previously mentioned, the best way to attain success is at the cross-section of health, wealth, self and happiness; this multi-faceted, well-rounded version of success is the ideal way to live a truly fulfilling life.

But how should you go about getting a good idea of where this cross-section is for you? Part of the process involves learning to balance all the elements of your life. Each aspect is important in its own way, and while you may find that you prioritize one aspect over another, all of them should have a place in your ideal future. Another part of the process is deciding what exactly your ideal future is. How much money do you want to have? Do you simply want enough to live securely, or are you seeking the comfort that excess wealth provides? What does your future family look like, and what sort of lifestyle do you enjoy together? Do you seek out travel, or are you happy getting to know the ins and outs of your hometown? Picture what a perfect day of your ideal future would look like, and from now on, do everything in your power to achieve that future.

Reverse Engineer Your Plan

The Reverse Success Plan is a tool for understanding and breaking down the path to success into manageable steps. Like setting goals, the plan involves picturing the final outcome and working backward to devise the road to reaching that outcome. Its basis might sound familiar to you as a typical job interview question – where do you see yourself in five years? Of course, there is no potential employer to sway your answer, so consider your response carefully and remain honest, yet optimistic. If you were able to accomplish all of your goals from this moment onward, what would your life look like in five years? The answer to this question can provide you guidance on how to proceed and exactly what goals you should focus on achieving. Work backward from your five-year goal to reverse engineer the steps to success.

To show you how to construct a Reverse Success Plan, first try it on a smaller scale. Say you wanted to go on a holiday to Bali, Indonesia. Success to you would mean enjoying your trip, traveling safely and having ample spending money to participate in activities at your leisure without too many restrictions.

If we were to reverse engineer the process and work backward from there, what steps would you need to take to achieve that goal? You would likely need to calculate and allocate an amount of funds every week leading up to your holiday that you could incrementally grow or compound so you have enough money to purchase the necessities of the trip. This may include your airfare, travel insurance, accommodation, transport and allocate funds towards food and entertainment. Let me provide you with a practical example.

End Goal:
7 Day Holiday to Bali on October 15th.

The steps we would take using the reverse success method could include:

Step 1: Determine the amount of money that you require for all expenses. Eg. $3,500

Step 2: The holiday is planned in 8 months, but you need to make all your bookings two months in advance, so the expenses are not placed on a credit card accruing interest. You therefore calculate that $3,500 / 24 weeks (6 months) = $146 p/week

Step 3: Establish a separate Holiday Bank Account that you promise 'NOT TO TOUCH'.

Step 4: Arrange for an automatic bank transfer of $146 p/week to your Bali Holiday Account the day you get paid so it is not missed or used for other general expenses.

Step 5: When the amount hits $3,500 in the 6th month, you then make the required bookings utilising the allocated funds either online or through a travel agent.

Step 6: Two weeks prior to departure, confirm all arrangements so you are relaxed and ready to go including your transfers to and from the airport.

Step 7: October 15th – Departure Day!

Applying this method to a short term or even long-term goal can help you visualize the steps you need to achieve with much greater success. Neglecting to establish a Reverse Success Plan can leave you uncertain on how to proceed and keep success firmly out of your grasp, so it is integral to plan your actions. Utilizing it to your advantage is in your best interest. To make your Reverse Success Plan as effective as possible, make your end goal as clear and specific as you can so that you can thoroughly plot out the pathway to success. Imagine what your perfect version of your health, wealth, relationships, and overall life would be in every possible way so that you can understand what you can do today, in this very moment, to get closer to those goals.

A Personal Commitment

Being completely committed to your goals is the only way to see them through to the end. If your resolve is weak, tough times and uncertain futures will keep you from moving forward. It is only through relentless commitment that you can guarantee that you will succeed in your endeavors. Make a personal commitment to yourself that you will keep trying and see everything through to its end result, no matter how long you have to work at it to see results; so long as you are dedicated and committed, you will find the success you are searching for.

Another great way to achieve a goal is by introducing automations that are an excellent 'set and forget' strategy. The financial automation example of the holiday to Bali is the perfect example. If the automation isn't established, imagine how hard it would be to find $3,500 in cash at the last minute, worse still, placing the expenses on a credit card and spending the next 12 months paying for your holiday when it is now a long distant memory plus additional interest.

Enthusiasm vs. Commitment to Achieve Your Goals

Be careful not to confuse enthusiasm with commitment. Though the two terms initially sound similar, they are actually very different from each other. "The word enthusiasm indicates intense excitement," but that excitement tends to be only situational and can even be faked when necessary (Vocabulary.com, n.d., para. 1). While enthusiasm may provide a temporary boost in productivity, it is unsustainable and will fade once true difficulty appears. Commitment, on the other hand, is a weightier decision to fully dedicate yourself to a goal or cause that cannot be faked. Before you commit, think carefully. A commitment obligates you to do something. When you make a commitment, you must be completely prepared to follow through on your promise.

To better understand the differences between the two, consider the example of visiting the gym. If you are merely enthusiastic about going to the gym, you likely lack a good sense of your goals and desired outcomes. You may have simply decided to exercise more often as part of a New Year's resolution or a similarly spontaneous decision. Enthusiasm tends to die off around the second week when you are feeling sore, and you begin to make excuses that allow you to skip the gym until you are no longer exercising at all. If you are truly committed to going to the gym, however, you will push through the excuses and stick to your regimen, aided by a greater sense of focus and a sense of clarity when it comes to knowing what you want to achieve. Real commitment involves a conscious decision not to give up when pushing forward becomes inconvenient and it allows you to continue working towards your goals. To aid your commitment and longevity towards pursuing a goal, it requires the introduction of incremental daily habits. This will be covered in **Step 3**.

An Essential Starting Point

Following the above instructions from Step 1 are essential for achieving what you really want in life with the development of the right mindset. They provide the rock-solid foundation upon which you build the rest of the pathway to success, and without a strong foundation, every step you take could be an uncertain one. That is why it is so necessary to develop the success mindset, put limiting beliefs behind you, understand your own conditions for success, and devote yourself to pushing back against any challenges you may encounter. By starting on the right foot, you will develop the positive, committed mindset necessary to attract everything you need to achieve your goals and kick-start your new life.

Chapter summary:

- Develop a success mindset and make the commitment to change
- Ultimately, you are the one most responsible for your journey in life
- Letting self-doubt infect your thoughts is a recipe for disaster
- Use goals as waypoints towards complete success
- Take the time to understand what success means to you
- Reverse engineer your goals to outline the path to success
- Understand that failure will occur, but that failure is an opportunity, not a roadblock

Step 2

DR. ACTION
Goal Setting

Without action, nothing ever happens. If there is one single phrase I want you to remember from this book, let it be this: *"The decisions you make and the actions you take will define your success."* Simply thinking about all the ways you can proceed will not actually change your state. You can read all the self-help books you like, attend countless motivational seminars and conferences, listen to podcasts and enrol in as many online courses as you want, but without ever taking the next step into action and putting that newfound knowledge into action, you will remain idle. What separates the high achievers from those struggling to get by and those with influence, simply comes down to the decisions you make and the actions you take, as they are what define the path you carve towards your ultimate success.

The key to taking action is not just goal setting, but goal development. Following the proper steps of goal development and implementation will show you how to get moving and accomplish your goals rather than waiting around for them. The most effective way of following a clear and practical goal setting process is through a process that I designed exclusively for my clients called **DR. ACTION™.** This system has revolutionized goal setting since its inception in early 2019.

DR. ACTION™

Dr Action is a carefully crafted acronym that was designed to provide a helpful and memorable way to guide my clients through the goal-setting process. You too now have access to this exclusive method. Let's take a look at what each of the letters stands for in DR. ACTION.

D is for **DREAM BIG** – Don't shy away from dreaming big and really challenging yourself. Find clarity on what you want and really push yourself to see significant, sweeping change in your life.

R is for **RELEVANT** – Any goal you set should be important to you. Figure out the reasons why a goal really matters to you specifically to keep motivation high for completing your path and pushing through the inevitable challenges.

A is for **ACTION** – Take immediate action by identifying and writing down your big goals. Consistently motivate yourself to keep moving forward whenever possible.

C is for **COORDINATES** – Develop a plan for achieving your goals that includes a series of actionable steps that will bring you closer to the finish line.

T is for **TIME** – Establish specific and realistic time frames for your goals. Consider how long it will most likely take you to complete a goal and do your best to stick to your time limit.

I is for **IMPLEMENT** – Follow through with any commitments you make. Start working immediately, and do not stop until you see results and achieve your desired outcome.

O is for **OPPORTUNITY** – Always be on the lookout for any potential opportunities, even when they cloak themselves in the guise of failures. Opportunity is everywhere.

N is for **NOW** – Begin your journey now. Your biggest dreams can become a reality, but only if you start working towards them right this moment.

The DR. ACTION™ plan is a foolproof method for setting and achieving effective goals, as well as an invaluable part of your toolset. Each of these steps will be expanded upon in further detail so that you can make the most of this plan for success and begin to see results in no time at all.

A Brief Outline of Goal Setting

Before we commence, I have outlined the six basic foundation steps that will form our structure of goals and the background of Dr ACTION.

Step 1:

Initial development of your goals

What do you want to achieve, and why do you want to achieve it? This is the time to dream big and decide what goals you are going to pursue. What will help you live your dream life? Identify what you are going to try to accomplish and what steps you need to take to get there.

Step 2:

Write your goals down

Writing down your goals allows you to commit them to memory and have an easier time visualizing them. Studies have actually proven that you are over 40% more likely to achieve your goals if they are actually physically written down! Though you may have written many goals, narrow them down to your top five most important ones so that you can efficiently focus on achieving those with a specific approach rather than an overly broad one. You should also include a date by which you will achieve your goals to give you a sense of perspective and urgency that encourages you to take action sooner rather than later.

Step 3:

Develop your destination map

To achieve your ideal results, you are going to need a map to guide you. First, have a good idea of what your end goal will look like. Then, use the reverse engineer method to work backward from your goals to plot out the path to success. This route will serve as your destination map that will guide you every day until you reach your end goal.

Step 4:

Daily visualization

Return to the list of goals you have written down every single day. Read them out loud so that you begin every day with a reminder of where you are headed. This will allow you to subconsciously always be thinking about ways to achieve these goals, and you will notice any opportunities you encounter throughout the day that will get you closer to success. The more these thoughts consume your subconscious, the higher your level of success to achieve your goals.

Step 5:

Establish daily habits

Chaining together positive daily habits that take you closer to your goal will help you make progress every day. Supportive habits create the system and structure you require to develop the best version of yourself both physically and mentally.

Step 6:

Take action every single day

Every day should help you move closer to your goals. Any day that you fail to complete your daily habits and goals is a day of lost opportunity.

Ensuring each day is filled with activity is the best way to finally achieve your goals and be successful.

Identify two to three actions to complete each day, and ensure that you complete those actions by the day's end. You will proceed closer and closer to your goal without even noticing how far you have gotten.

Tip: Purchase 'The Daily Goal Tracker' resource that has been recommended by Brian Tracy.

Testimonial by Brian Tracy: *"This amazing book, 'The Daily Goal Tracker', is an extraordinary resource that shows you how to set your goals, organize your life, double and triple your income, and achieve more, faster, than you ever thought possible."*

<u>DREAM BIG</u>

Gaining Clarity on What You Truly Want

The first stage of goal setting should involve visualizing what you really want to achieve. The power of visualization is not to be overlooked. Seeing yourself as someone capable and ready for success creates an inner motivation to strive for your goals and dreams and promotes positive thinking, which will help you stay on track for success. It has also been found to teach your brain to recognize what resources it will need to help you succeed in reaching your goals so that you are always seeking new opportunities. But knowing how to visualize in the most beneficial way is essential for getting the most motivation out of your imagination. Be bold and think big. The goals you settle on will need to be important enough to drive you closer to your destination every day, and you cannot accomplish much if your goals are as average as getting a few cents extra as a raise. The future you imagine in this step will have to push you through the most trying times, so they should be big and important enough that you remain resilient in the face of any obstacles you may encounter.

Still, you do not want to be entirely unrealistic in your goals either. Shooting for something entirely impossible to accomplish in a reasonable timeframe can be as demoralizing as a goal you do not feel passionate about. To achieve a happy balance between the two extremes, think about where you would like to be in the next year, the next five years, and the next ten years. Set aside some time and a quiet location to think about your ideal future with no distractions. I suggest hybrids between meditation and visualization which involve focusing on key sounds and smells as you visualize your future. These should be completed at a minimum of once [per] day for 15-20 minutes," and for an added sense of consistency, you may even like to do one as you drift off to sleep every night. Think broadly during the initial visualization, then fill in as many details as you can so you know exactly what you want. Next, return to the goals you have identified and attach a reason or purpose behind each one. This will help you ensure you can visualize with absolute clarity and properly motivate yourself.

You should also have a sense of balance between the different goals you identify during the process of visualization. Be sure to cover all aspects of your life, including the areas of health, wealth, self-improvement, and sources of happiness like family and relationships.

"Whatever you can do, or dream you can do, begin it. Boldness has genius, power and magic in it."
Johann Wolfgang von Goethe
(1749-1832)

Health Goals

Health-centric goals should involve ways to improve both your physical and mental health. A healthy body and mind will provide you with the energy you need to keep moving forward and chasing new opportunities, feeding back into your ability to achieve your goals. Ask yourself these questions when deciding on the health goals that work best for you.

- What will I do to get or stay fit?
- What exercise should I incorporate into my daily schedule?
- How can I make more time for mental or physical exercises?
- How many days each week should exercise?

Wealth Goals

Wealth goals are ways to improve your financial situation and achieve security and comfort rather than money-related anxiety. They should focus on not only liquid assets like money in your bank account but also non-liquid assets like your housing situation. Consider the following questions when setting your wealth goals.

- Where do I want to be living?
- What investments do I want to own?
- How much money would it take to be living comfortably?
- What passive income can I generate so my money is 'working for me'?
- Is there a savings or financial goal I want to achieve?

Self and Happiness Goals

Self-goals include self-improvement and personal development goals. They are opportunities to improve yourself so that you can live a more fulfilling life. Happiness goals are about achieving whatever makes you happy in life and can include anything from hobbies to new relationships and starting or supporting a family. Keep the following questions in mind when you determine your 'self and happiness' goals.

- What career path do I want to be in? Do I want to start my own business?
- What skills do I want to improve in? How will I acquire my new knowledge?
- Is there a destination I wish to travel to?
- Do I have any relationship goals?
- Is there a goal I have in mind for my community and its members?
- Is there a special item I want to purchase as a reward for achieving my other goals?
- What one skill would I most benefit from? How would it change my life if I learned it?

<u>RELEVANT</u>

Make It Personal to You

Your goals need to matter, and they need to matter to you. So many people spend their lives living for someone else's sake and only pursuing things because it is what someone else wants. We have all heard of the person who goes to law school or studied for years to be a doctor to impress their parents and make money but in exchange have repressed their true passions. These jobs can be great aspirational roles, but if they do not truly interest you, then don't waste your life following someone else's dreams.

In order to establish a real drive to get things done, your goals need to be big dreams that you are personally invested in. Stop living for other people and start living for yourself. Think of the reasons why achieving a specific goal would make you happy and what it would allow you to do. Ask yourself what positive impact it will have for you first and then consider how it may help those around you who you care about as well. A great goal should produce a sort of healthy obsession with completing it, and this is *impossible* if you choose something you do not truly want. Many people drop out of college because the degree program they chose wasn't something they really enjoyed, so they were unable to focus on the coursework and ultimately gave up on it. Don't be the one that let your dreams evaporate; choose goals that you would give anything to achieve and the motivation to follow through with them will come naturally.

How to Successfully Support Relevant Goals

Setting and achieving your goals requires making an ongoing commitment and continually investing your time and energy. You will need to take steps every day to make progress. Therefore, you will have the best chance of success if you deeply and passionately care about whatever you decide on. Additionally, goals need to have allocated resources. Whether that's time or money or both. Typically, goals involve dedicated time, effort and focus. Taking stock of your current and available resources will help you identify the goals that are most likely to bear fruit should you choose to pursue them. Being able to understand what resources are required for a goal will help you identify a reasonable time frame when deciding on a deadline. Anything important to you is worth doing, so if you are truly dedicated to a cause, you will be able to allocate the time and other resources that achieving it requires.

ACTION

Become Committed and Take Action

Once you've dreamed up your goals, the next step is to take immediate action. Now is not the time for procrastinating and dragging your feet. You must start today to see any change in your life. Even if you don't think you can accomplish any big steps right away, start with the small things and work your way up to the more challenging tasks. If you were trying to bake a cake without any prior experience, you wouldn't start by mixing ingredients blindly; instead, you would start by looking up a recipe and taking a trip to the grocery store and then by following the steps that will provide a successful outcome. You can tackle any goal in a similar way. Start by gathering the necessary information and connections, and then begin implementing the newfound knowledge and resources starting with the easy stuff and working your way up to the harder stuff. The momentum you gain from completing even the simplest of tasks will carry you through to tackling the bigger challenges. If you hesitate and allow your momentum to fade without taking action, you could jeopardize your chances of long-term success. If you have been guilty of procrastinating before, use this moment that can change your life!

> *"Good thoughts are no better than good dreams if you don't follow through."*
> *Ralph Waldo Emerson (1803-1882)*

Write Your Goals Down

Taking action begins with writing your goals down and reminding yourself of them regularly. Look at your goals at the start of every day, and identify two or three things you can do each day to take yourself a little closer to achieving them. When you keep your goals in the forefront of your mind at all times, you notice any possible opportunity that presents itself throughout the day. Your subconscious will pick up on anything relevant, and many more so-called "coincidences" will appear once you are really paying attention.

The process of writing your goals down is like entering into an agreement with yourself. Think of it like writing out a contract in which you identify what you want to achieve and the date by which you want to achieve it by. Having agreed to this contract, you are now accountable for fulfilling it. You must take action to follow through on the contract and keep your promises to yourself.

You may start writing and come up with pages and pages of potential goals, to the point where it is overwhelming. Trying to split your attention between so many possibilities can leave you uncertain as to where to even begin. If this occurs, narrow your focus to your top 5 – 10 goals to achieve in the next 12 months. Choose goals that will be achievable within the given time limit, even if they will require a good deal of elbow grease, and those that will give you the confidence and strong foundation to begin working towards your overarching ten-year goals. This way, each goal you achieve will carry you closer to your long-term goals for much bigger successes.

Motivating Yourself

Getting started can be one of the most challenging steps you take on your journey. How do you motivate yourself to become an active participant in your life rather than a passive observer? Different strategies will work for different people, and there are quite a few methods you can use. One is to break down a difficult task into easier steps (refer **Step 1 –** Reverse Engineering), which allows you to start with confidence boosters that give you the skills to tackle harder ordeals. Another is learning how to manage the presence of distractions in your life. Life is full of distractions, but you should know how to remove yourself from these situations when you know that you need to be taking action instead of the distraction of social media or YouTube. Recent studies suggest that the average period of time that someone can focus on a singular task is 45 seconds! Cutting out distractions that only serve to keep you from your goals will provide you with more time to do the things that matter. Additionally, it can help to identify an activity that helps to replenish your energy levels when they are feeling drained. This can be anything from a quick exercise session, to playing with a pet, to listening to your favorite energetic song. Whatever you choose, it should refresh you and help you think more clearly to be focused on the task at hand. What works for you depends on what your best conditions for work are. Figure out how to keep yourself moving forward when times are tough so that you can revitalize yourself and continue taking action, whether you are conquering a particularly challenging hurdle or just starting out.

<u>COORDINATES</u>
Develop Your Plan to Achieve Your Goals

Plotting the course for achieving your goals is a bit like being a ship captain voyaging into treacherous and unknown seas. Without careful planning and a way to chart your course, you risk running aground or getting lost at sea. However, so long as you take the proper precautions to plan out your journey, you can avoid the risk of early failure.

Developing your plan is a vital element for achieving any goal. Without knowing how to arrive at your destination, how will you know what you need to do to get there? Understanding each step of your journey allows you to implement the habits and actions that will bring you closer to success in your life. It can also keep you from leading yourself astray and wasting time on actions that do not bring you closer to your goal. Proper planning ensures that the actions you spend your time and effort on really matter and each one aids you in getting where you want to go.

"If your train is on the wrong track, every station you come to is the wrong station."
Bernard Malamud (1914-1986)

How to Chart Your Course

Many people falter in goal setting because they believe that simply writing their goals down is enough. They set the goals aside without any more in-depth thought, and as a result, they forget about them. This is a sure-fire way to significantly limit your opportunities and muddy the waters of your path to success. The best way to counteract this "set and forget" tendency is to thoroughly and clearly plan out the route you will take to reach your goal.

Your plan will depend on the size and difficulty of your goal. A short-term goal may only require five steps, while a stretch goal may involve 50. Work backward from your destination to devise steps (refer to *reverse engineering your goals* – Step 1) that will naturally build upon each other, and think of each step as a new coordinate in your voyage that will lead you to the next one. You will also need to decide what you need to change or introduce into your life and the daily routine and habits to help you achieve your goal. What parts of your everyday life are keeping you from achieving success, and how can you alter them to better suit your needs? Identify the changes you need to make and plot out a path for changing them, once again starting from the finished product and working backward. This should leave you with manageable, bite-sized steps that serve as a completed map when viewed as a whole.

An important note that I would like to highlight though is that it is certainly not possible, nor would I expect that you could know all the sequential steps or actions you need to take to achieve your goals. Along your journey, you will need to stop, review, modify, pivot and then continue your plan every few months to accommodate any unexpected challenges you have encountered. As long as you have focus on the end point and review your plan often, the steps will come into focus for you to follow.

To illustrate this, *I would like to use the analogy of crossing a small stream using a narrow log. When you cross the log, you should keep your eyes ahead with laser like focus and your arms out wide. If you do this, you will naturally take the right steps, maintain your balance and continue to move forward. You will also neutralize your fear of toppling into the cold water. If you look directly down at your feet, you will not only lose your momentum and focus, but also your balance and confirm your worst fears of falling in. Keep your eyes ahead and on your goal!*

"Obstacles are those frightful things you see when you take your eyes off your goal."

Henry Ford (1863-1947)

<u>TIME</u>
Develop Deadlines for Your Goals

Set a specific timeline for each goal you plan to achieve. By setting a date by which a goal must be accomplished, you can begin to apply the timeframe to each step in the process. This will give you a better idea of how long each leg of your journey should take, help you notice when you are falling behind, and keep you motivated to stay on track. You are in full control of the speed of your journey, but you should pick timeframes that are encouraging while not being overwhelming in the amount of work they are asking you to do.

Allocating a time limit to a goal helps your subconscious prioritize the actions needed to complete the goal. Rather than being a nebulous future event, creating a timeline takes your goal from something that will happen in the future and moves it into the present. This means that the pressing need to complete the next goal is ever-present. You may be tempted to spend excessive time on leisure activities, but your brain will keep reminding you that your deadline is fast approaching, which will make wasting time much less appealing. You will feel accountable for finishing your tasks rather than allowing time to slip past you unused. An effective endpoint keeps you moving forward and helps you understand how far you have come and how far you still have to go.

Long-Term and Short-Term Timelines

There are a few differences in setting deadlines for short-term goals versus more involved goals. Those that can be accomplished in less than a year should be somewhat more in-depth with each part of the process having its own timeline and setps, as you have a reasonably accurate idea of what your life will look like at each stage of the process. Try to shift your deadlines as little as possible. For more long-term goals, such as those that you assign a five year or greater deadline to, focus on the smaller goals that will help you achieve the larger ones. You can adjust your long-term timelines when necessary as you go, as a lot is likely to change over the course of five years. Set yourself up for future success by concentrating on what you can achieve in the short-term.

IMPLEMENT
Take the Action to Start

It's time to implement all of the planning and knowledge you have accumulated so far. This is when you finally lift the safety seal that covers the launch switch. Make the commitment to achieving your goals official and begin putting in the actual work to get things done. Everything you have done up to this moment has been preparatory work that will help you succeed during this step. Taking the plunge and moving forward with your goals will put you on the express path to success. Not everyone takes this first step, but most people who reach the implementation phase and make the commitment to following their carefully laid plans have an incredibly high chance of achieving their goals so long as they stay the course and see it through to the end.

This is the time to begin implementing the supportive daily habits that build the system and structures that will significantly increase your chances of success.

Avoiding Procrastination

Attempts to implement your plans can be stopped dead in their tracks by the dreaded procrastination. It is important to remember not to delay your plans and avoid common procrastination pitfall traps. You can prevent delays by deciding to plan each day in advance and set priorities on your activities so you are completing what is most important first. Brian Tracy says "get up, get going, and get started". Planning and taking actions that follow through on your plans is the best cure for procrastination. If misfortune and lousy timing plague you and keep you from moving forward, simply focus on doing the best work you can today. You may not be able to accomplish miraculous growth every day, but you can make some progress, no matter how small. Any progress is better than none at all.

"Realize what you really want. It stops you from chasing butterflies and puts you to work digging gold."
William Moulton Marsden (1893-1947)

<u>OPPORTUNITY</u>
Recognize when it is presented to you

Opportunities are always passing by, but it's up to each of us to recognize and seize them. If you don't take an opportunity, it will be passed onto someone else, and you will miss out on whatever benefit it would have given you. To be sure you take full advantage of opportunities, you must be aware of them at all times. Frequently checking your goals and committing them to memory will help your subconscious recognize chances to further your progress when they appear.

"Opportunities pass by; they don't pause."
Anon

Opportunities can present themselves in all sorts of weird and wonderful ways. You could run into someone you haven't seen in five years that helps you connect with someone who needs your services. You might read an advertisement for a seminar on achieving one of your goals. An expert in your field might visit your area only once every few years; if you do not jump onto this opportunity, you will miss out on excellent advice and have a harder time reaching your goals. Recognizing and learning to say yes to new opportunities, even those that may at first appear intimidating, is a key step in achieving success.

Let me share with you a short story:

Two salesmen from competing shoe companies are asked to travel halfway across the world to an underdeveloped region of Africa to investigate the expansion of their respective shoe businesses. They both spend a few days at the location and return to their managers with their business report. One salesman reports back that there is simply no market for shoes as nobody wears them. The 2nd salesman comes back super excited and reports to his manager that there is a huge opportunity as nobody wears shoes!

As you can see, it depends how you interpret those opportunities that are presented to you and one opportunity may simply move to another if you allow it to pass.

Playing the Odds

You may be under the impression that opportunities are simply luck-based. While it is true that they may appear in your life through chance, there are ways you can play the odds and increase your chances of success. Networking and making a name for yourself are great ways to attract opportunities as more people hear about what you are accomplishing. You should put in any necessary preparatory work ahead of time so that you are ready when an opportunity comes knocking. Additionally, you need to remain open and aware of the opportunities that do present themselves and take action when needed. If you need to make a follow-up phone call or reach out to someone first, then do not let these actions fall by the wayside in favour of waiting for easier opportunities. They may never come, and you will find that another lucky person will take advantage of the one you let slip by.

"Luck is what happens when preparation meets opportunity."
Seneca the Elder (c. 55 BC-39 AD)

NOW

Eliminate Procrastination from Your Mindset

The final step of DR. ACTION is to act right now. You've established a plan and put in the preparatory work to complete the seven prior goal setting steps. Now it is time to actually go out and achieve those goals. Put everything you have learned into action and do it now rather than letting another day pass you by.

There is no better time to start than today. Let your momentum from completing the past steps carry you through to fully integrating goal-setting practices and a success mindset into your life. It will take significant dedication, daily effort, a healthy dose of courage, and a commitment to fighting back against your limiting beliefs with ferocity. But remember that you have set your sights on these goals for a reason and achieving them will be worth every hardship you experience in the meantime. Your strong motivation and powerful mindset will carry you through to the finish line.

Write Down Your Goals Today

Remember, when writing your goals to note the following:

1. The **SPECIFIC DATE** you wish to achieve the goal by.
2. Your Reason **WHY** this goal is important to you
3. Dream **BIG** but not unrealistic
4. Be specific so you have absolute **CLARITY**.

12 Month - Health Goals

1.
2.
3.

12 Month - Wealth Goals

1.
2.
3.

<u>12 Month - Self & Happiness Goals</u>

1.

2.

3.

Chapter summary:

- Learn and abide by the steps of DR. ACTION™
- Don't be afraid to dream big and push yourself to achieve your goals
- Set goals that incorporate elements of health, wealth, self, and happiness
- Make your goals relevant to your desires and personally fulfilling
- Take action whenever possible
- Write goals down to keep your subconscious thinking about them at all times
- Create a foolproof, in-depth plan for reaching short term goals
- Set deadlines that are appropriate for the type and difficulty of each goal
- Keep your eyes and mind focused ahead and don't look down. You will lose your balance.
- Implement the skills you have learned from DR ACTION™ to improve your productivity
- Always seek opportunities and start saying yes to them when they appear

"Your life is up to you. Life provides the canvas: you do the painting." Anon

Step 3

Structures and Systems:

Building Supportive Daily Habits

The overarching structure of your life should be one that allows growth and development to proceed naturally from your daily activities. Even when you are not consciously thinking about them, the frequent habits you engage in, cause you to develop mental and physical systems that can make your life easier or harder. Engage in the right daily habits and beneficial actions and many will begin to occur autonomously with little extra input necessary. Engage in the wrong ones, and you can sabotage your productivity with a shaky foundation that crumbles under pressure. Your daily habits determine what kind of a mindset you hold and what you can accomplish, so habits that are supportive of your goals and get you where you need to be each day are an absolute must.

When considering what habits would be most effective for you, first learn what habits the most successful people in your field practice. Then, do your best to emulate those habits. I strongly believe in the 90/10 rule; that is, 10 percent of the big winners are separated from 90 percent of everyone else. The average person, part of the 90 percent that reach low to middling success in their lives, puts in the average amount of work. They perform the most common actions to achieve their goals, but they are unlikely to commit themselves to anything extreme. The remaining 10 percent, on the other hand, do what the 90 percent are unwilling to do. They make the big sacrifices, take the risky plays, and above all else, follow the most beneficial daily habits that others might see as too drastic. You will only achieve extreme success by making extreme plays, and that means shaking the habits of the 90 percent. If you want to lose weight, follow the exercise and dietary habits of those who have lost the most weight. If you want to start a business, learn what the biggest names did to get their start-ups off the ground and do the same. Whatever your goal, if you emulate the big winners in your field and consistently go above and beyond the average, you will find your own success. In summary, "you need to do more of the things that the average person isn't prepared to do!"

Reprogramming Your Brain

Over time, your brain is programmed to perform in different ways, depending on the experiences you have had and the actions you have taken in the past. Constantly reinforcing a behavior, whether positive or negative, instructs your brain to perform the same action or think along the same lines again and again. We are more comfortable with what we know, so without a conscious decision to do otherwise, we will take the path we have followed before and this is usually the path of least resistance. Creating supportive daily habits reprograms your brain away from the harmful actions and reinforces the beneficial ones. After sticking to positive habits for a <u>minimum</u> of 60 days, you will notice that things begin to automate themselves as you start to develop a significant shift in your mindset and behavior. Your newly reprogrammed brain will start to ditch bad habits and cultivate productive ones in as little as 30 days.

Generally, habits take about 60 to 90 days of implementation to be fully integrated into your brain. This can vary depending on the *'frequency'* of the activity, but more often than not, you will need to perform a habit for an extended period before it becomes an unconscious process. Repetition is key. This is also true of unlearning bad habits. Unfortunately, it takes as long to unlearn a bad habit as it does to learn a good one, but you can train yourself out of any habits that might be holding you back with enough time and dedication. Save yourself the time by avoiding developing bad habits in the first place and doing things the right way the first time rather than taking shortcuts or losing focus.

Good and Bad Habits

What differentiates a good habit from a bad one? Simply put, a good habit is anything that helps you in building a better version of yourself. Good habits help you unlock your potential and meet your goals. They may help you improve your knowledge and education, your fitness, your physical or mental health, your wealth, or any number of other positive goals. They may also make you happier, but in the more fulfilled sense that comes from completed goals and realized aspirations rather than the fleeting sort of happiness that comes from a single leisure activity.

Bad habits, on the other hand, are habits that stand in the way of your goals. They are detrimental to your growth and only restrict you from all you could otherwise achieve. Bad habits are often time wasters like television binges and oversleeping. Social media is another common time sink that can prevent productivity. They are also activities with negative impacts on your health, such as overeating, lack of exercise, smoking, and excessive drinking. If a habit isn't helping you to achieve your goals, then it is hurting you and you should take the necessary steps to replace it as soon as possible. Though you may give up the initial small bursts of false happiness that come with eating junk food or watching your third basketball game in a row, you will exchange them for something much more real and concrete with a notable impact on your life.

Your Why Factor

To develop good daily habits, you need to understand what motivates you and why it does so. An equally strong and supportive reason for each strong and supportive habit will ensure that you keep doing the habit for as long as necessary. If you understand why something is important and why you want to get it done, you will spend less time fighting with yourself and simply buckle down and do it. For example, if you are unemployed and seeking a job, your resolve to keep sending in applications may waver after the first few rejections. You may ask yourself why you're even bothering, and as a result, looking for new jobs to apply for will start to fade from your daily habits. You can counteract this by having a firm, clear idea of the answer to your question. What you will gain in the form of financial security and doing something you're passionate about likely far outweighs the reflex desire to give up. Remembering why you care about what you are doing and how it will help you can motivate you to finish any task.

Everything you are doing should matter in one way or another. Whether you enjoy the task itself or you are simply pursuing the outcome, you should understand the reasons behind your actions. There are so many distractions that make it easy to fill our lives up with things that don't really matter to us. The trick is to ask ourselves how we spend less time doing unimportant things and more time doing the things we love to do. Always question what your why factor is for each new activity that enters your life. In what way will it benefit you to do this task? If you cannot come up with an answer, then reconsider if it is a task you need to complete or not.

Changing the Game

Having a firm grasp on your why factor of every decision you make can help you revolutionize your life and really make a connection with others as you achieve your goal. It allows you to access and stick to daily habits that are total game changers for you. Without knowing your why factor, you could keep putting off taking the plunge on starting that new business or beginning that new exercise routine. You will remain uncertain about really committing yourself to it because you do not understand why it matters. Once you do, it will be easy to take that final step and really pursue a big change. These are the types of decisions that help you grow as a person and alter the course of your life.

"My own experience has taught me this: if you wait for the perfect moment when all is safe and assured it may never arrive. Mountains will not be climbed, races won, or lasting happiness achieved."
Maurice Chevalier (1888-1972)

Knowing your 'why factor' can also inspire those around you and rally them into support. This can be a small group of family and friends who understand your goals and are eager to help you pursue them, or it can be thousands of new customers who empathize with your mission and lend you their support. You may notice that if a brand supports a cause you care about, you are much more likely to maintain brand loyalty. The same is true of others when you have your own personal brand. If you are looking for a loyal, supportive following, remember that "when we align emotionally with our customers and clients, our connection is much stronger and more meaningful than any affiliation based on features and benefits. That's what starting with the WHY is all about" (Simon Sinek – Start with Why). Fighting for a cause will accrue more loyalty than almost any other action. Knowing and sharing your why factor will attract other like-minded people to support you so that you can inspire real change.

Incremental Changes

If you want to see MASSIVE changes, you need to ease your way into your new habits rather than making drastic changes right away. To ensure you can maintain a habit over time, you need to minimize resistance to keep continual change a sustainable option. For example, if you wanted to start waking up at 5:00 am, and you usually get up at 6:30 am, simply starting by setting the alarm for 5:00 will leave you groggy at best and sleeping through your alarm at worst. It is much easier for your body if you wake up 5 - 10 minutes earlier each day and slowly acclimatize yourself to the new schedule. Setting new habits operates similarly; you are more likely to establish and stick with a habit if you let yourself ease into it. I see this process as similar to a deep-water diver. If the diver doesn't become accustomed to the pressures of the ocean on either their way down or way up, they can develop a severe condition called 'The Bends' due to internal decompression issues in their system that can be fatal. The moral of this analogy: introduce change slowly!

"High aspirations start with what you want to achieve in the future and simply working back from there to develop the required habits, principles, goals and mindset."
Romney Nelson

The ultimate plan is to start with small changes, and that paves the way for much larger ones. Without the development of strong and consistent daily habits, you will be unable to commit yourself to the daily habits that allow you to achieve success, but this does not mean pushing yourself out of your comfort zone right away. Never expect to adopt a habit immediately, especially when it makes a big impact. Starting good habits takes more work than starting bad ones, as "good habits are hard to form but easy to live with. Bad habits, on the other hand, are easy to form but hard to live with. In either case, you develop either good or bad habits as a result of your repeated choices, decisions, and behaviors" (Brian Tracy, 2017, p. 4). Repeatedly choosing to give up work time or put off an important activity sets you up to sabotage yourself, while incrementally fixing your bad habits ensures you can continue to improve and grow.

To understand the benefits of starting small when building up strong habits, let's look at another example. Say you are not a swimmer, but you want to train for a .6-mile (1 km) swim. If you started trying to swim .6 miles every day with no prior training, you would exhaust yourself every time and likely become discouraged due to a lack of progress. If instead, you began at two laps and added just one more lap to your practice each day, you could comfortably push your limits without completely burning yourself out. Swimming only one extra lap is not an especially hard task, which makes it easy to add to your routine. An extra lap is around 25 m, so it would take you roughly 10 -12 weeks to build up to your ultimate goal. This may take a bit longer than short term, intense training sessions, but it forms the basis for continued practice and improvement while also minimizing the chance that you simply give up halfway through or suffer an overuse injury. That would ultimately be the worst possible outcome and could delay your progress for months. You can apply this strategy of incremental improvement to any habit or goal.

A Practical Application – Example of introducing an earlier wake up time and daily reading. The ultimate being a 5.30am wake-up and 30 minutes reading. Your priority is to introduce the change in small increments:

Application:
- Stagger your alarm times to be set 10 minutes earlier each week for 8 weeks. That way you will not even notice the difference. Remember, don't rush the change as this is a 'long-term' commitment so 8 weeks in the grand scale of the change is very insignificant.
- Introduce just 5 minutes of reading each morning for Week 1. Increase the reading by 5 minutes each week for 6 weeks = 30 minutes.

Tip: If you wanted to introduce morning AM exercise, provide as little resistance as possible to help you get going. This would include:

(i) having your exercise clothing and essentials neatly folded and ready for when you get out of bed. **(ii)** Have your podcast loaded and ready to play so you're not searching for a show/episode at 5.35am. **(iii)** Your **REASON** to introduce change via a new habit is essential as it needs to be strong enough to pull you out of bed each day regardless of rain, hail or shine. Be committed.

Layering Habits

You don't want to overwhelm yourself with too many new habits at once. Some people attempt to change many parts of their lives at once and end up overburdening themselves with expectations that they are unable to meet all at the same time. They end up jumping from one thing to another in rapid succession and never really feel comfortable with any individual habit. If these new habits are simply spread out over a longer period of time however, you can be much more successful at adopting them. If you are trying to start five new habits, it is more sensible to introduce one new habit each week. By the time five weeks are up, you will have five new habits that all fit comfortably into your existing schedule. By layering your new habits in this manner, you can determine which ones work and which ones do not. You can also make adjustments to how long you spend on each habit. If you try to include 30 minutes of informative reading into your schedule each day, but find that it intrudes too much upon your other responsibilities, you can easily identify the need to cut reading time down to 20 minutes rather than trying to sort through five different habits to find the problem. Keep making adjustments over the course of a week until you find the schedule that fits your lifestyle best.

Structuring Your Habits

You are more likely to stick to habits if they become part of your daily structure. An excellent way to guarantee this is to write your habits down as part of your schedule. Writing your habits down helps you to maintain accountability for completing them each day and keep them present in your mind as you work the habit into your daily life over a couple of months. List your habits like a to-do list, including the actions you need to complete as well as the times you should start and finish them. Keeping your habits organized in a to-do list is a great way to give your daily activities structure and ensure you complete everything you need to do each day.

Structuring your daily habits is an extremely important step for establishing a robust system. After a few weeks, you will start developing a dependency on completing them and become addicted to the amazing results they will help you achieve. The stronger your structure, the greater the chance that your habits will become ingrained into your routine and become automatic.

What Do Supportive Habits Look Like?

Powerful supportive habits should be aligned with your already established daily rhythms and structures. You should take a long-term view of your daily goals, as the habits you set here can be maintained long past achieving your initial goals. Supportive goals will help you achieve a wide variety of outcomes and carry you through into future successes.

The best supportive habits are at the core of achieving your goals because they will:

- Give you significant physical and mental improvements
- Increase your energy levels
- Bring you better focus or clarity
- Allow you to maintain your drive, focus, and commitment to your goals

Your morning routine sets the tone for the rest of your day, so you should start out on the right foot. Begin your day with supportive habits that will carry you through the rest of your day and set you up to make good choices throughout the day.

Let me provide you with a sneak peek into my personal supportive morning routine:

- *Rise early – 4:30 am*
  (6 Days p/week with Sunday as a sleep-in day)
- *Exercise with podcast audio*
  (fast pace walking or skipping) – 4:35 am
- *Healthy breakfast – 5:05 am*
- *150 Push Ups and 150 Sit Ups*
  (divided into 6 sets of 25) – 5.15 am
- *Meditation or visualization exercise – 5:35 am*

- *Daily Goal Reflection and list of my 3 key tasks/priorities – 6:00 am*
- *Reading for self-improvement– 6:15 am*
- *Shower – 6:45 am*
- *Start of the working day – 7.00am*

Please note that my habits were built incrementally over three - four months. If you are organized and continue to introduce new habits slowly your mind and body will adjust. Please also note that I do go to bed at 9.00pm and don't recommend anything less than 7 hours sleep p/night.

Exercise

Early exercise in the mornings helps wake you up and prepare your brain for the rest of the day. Very few people think about going for a jog first thing in the morning, but remember, leading the pack is about doing *more of the things the average person isn't prepared to do*. You can choose whatever kind of exercise appeals to you, whether you feel up to a morning jog or you prefer to use yoga to find your balance. High-intensity workouts are more beneficial for waking you up, so if you have trouble shaking off the sleepiness, go for something fast-paced. Even if you are reluctant to exercise, taking the time to do 5 minutes of intense skipping or sit-ups after getting out of bed really does make a difference. Exercise helps you to wake up early and make the most of the extra hours you have added to your schedule. You can spend this time starting work or investing in yourself and your fitness, both physically and mentally. As discussed in an earlier chapter, getting up just two hours earlier can add ten extra hours per week, 40 hours each month, and over three months of extra time each year. Without fully waking yourself up and calming your thoughts through exercise, you will miss out on all of this extra time.

Healthy Breakfast

You may have heard the saying that breakfast is the most important meal of the day. Some may disagree, but I'm a firm believer with my background as a graduate of Physical Education and qualified Personal Trainer that it helps to jumpstart your system and gets you ready to face the day. Breakfast starts your metabolism and gives you the energy you need to tackle anything that comes next. Because of this, you should never skip breakfast, especially if you are rising early to maximize your available time. You will need all the energy you can get to be as productive as possible, and failing to eat at the beginning of the day can lead to low energy levels and sluggishness. This is especially true if one of your goals is improved fitness. Without breakfast, your metabolism is slow to start, which can impede your efforts. Even eating a small breakfast on an especially busy day is better than none at all, though you should always strive to make a complete breakfast part of your daily schedule.

Some breakfasts are more conducive to productivity and high levels of energy than others. You should generally avoid big, heavy breakfasts full of fatty foods that can slow you down and aggravate health issues. This means skipping the sausage, bacon, and deep-fried hash browns or pancakes. You should also steer clear of breakfasts high in processed sugars like sweet cereals and some breakfast bars. While sugar may provide a temporary energy boost, it is not worth the potential crash you might experience later, nor is it worth the added sugar in your diet.

Instead, try to stick to fruits, vegetables, and whole grains. Incorporate fresh fruit by either slicing it up or blending it into a smoothie to take on the go. Utilize leafy greens like spinach, which are high in iron and nuts. Consider yogurt, porridge, or oatmeal in the mornings for something heartier that won't slow you down. Add grilled tomatoes or avocado to the meal for some non-artificial flavour. You should also include plenty of water in all of your meals, especially breakfast. A 500 ml glass of water is recommended to hydrate your system and replenish what you sweat out in your morning exercise. Make smart decisions with breakfast, and it will pay you back throughout the day.

Visualization or Meditation

The process of visualization goes hand-in-hand with a success mindset. Visualize your future successful self so that you remain motivated and focused on the task at hand. Doing so reinforces the supportive habits you have been learning and encourages you to keep going even when the changes you are making to your life seem difficult or frightening. The process of visualizing yourself achieving your goals "triggers hormones and synapses that make it easier to achieve those goals. When you've already envisioned the scenario, the real thing will feel familiar and much more feasible" rather than a far-off fantasy (Janeksela, 2018).

Once you have seen yourself accomplishing the tasks before you and living your best life, it seems much more likely that your reality will mimic your dreams. Your doubts melt away, allowing you to do whatever they were holding you back from without fear. Starting your day off with some visualization exercises can make the future seem that much closer to the present.

You may like to develop your unique variation of a Meditation (generally used to quiet and calm your mind using breathing exercises) or visualization as a supportive habit to add to your daily schedule. Meditating on your goals brings them to the forefront of your mind and can help you establish your reasons for pursuing a goal. Start by focusing on an area of your life, and then imagine the ideal version of yourself in that area. You may do this by considering a specific situation or even just by picturing an average day in your envisioned future. Explore your perfect future at your own pace, or use a guided meditation to help you focus. By the end of the meditation, you should feel more confident than ever about reaching your goals and all of the other good fortunes that doing so will give you.

Visualization and meditation can be practiced on their own, but they can also be combined with other activities where your brain is idle. This can be on your way to work, during your morning walk or jog, while making breakfast, or during any number of other activities. Combining these thought exercises with other activities helps you save time and make the most of each morning, doubling your productivity in the span of a few minutes.

Daily Goal Tracker

Recording your goals daily helps their imprint on your mind grow stronger and stronger. If you are always thinking about your goals, you will always be subconsciously looking for ways to achieve them. You should have a good idea of what goals you will prioritize for the day and which ones you still want to keep in the back of your mind. It is a good idea to set out a few smaller goals for the day that you want to accomplish as well as the big-picture goals that you want to continue thinking about while you are completing the smaller ones. You can help organize your daily goals by purchasing *The Daily Goal Tracker* that I developed specifically to help generate daily actions, record your gratitude and also conduct weekly and monthly reviews of your progress. It is an excellent goal-planning journal that is available from Amazon. *The Daily Goal Tracker* will help you organize each day so that you can get your goals done at the pace you set for yourself.

Your daily goal tracker should follow a similar structure each day. Start by writing out the top three actions you need to do today which will move you closer to your goals. These can be little things at first like making an important phone call to set up a meeting, reading a few more chapters of a book, or making more connections. As you progress with your goals and you have access to more resources, your daily actions will grow more ambitious. After you have written your three actions for the day, rewrite your top 10 goals that will influence every step you take that day. Read over your 12-month goals to ensure you are aligned with prioritization for the day and you are heading in the right direction. Having a solid, reliable, and well-organized daily goal tracker will ensure you are taking the right steps to get closer to completing your goals each day.

Reading, Podcasts, and Audiobooks

The average adult reads less than one nonfiction book per year. That is an incredible missed opportunity to continue learning and growing, especially considering the many convenient ways information is now available to us. Remember, success is about doing the things that the average person is unwilling to do; investing time into deepening your knowledge will put you leagues ahead of the average. Set some time aside to read a book, or listen to an informative podcast or audiobook in the car or while completing other idle activities. Did you know that if you allocated just two hours a day to personal education, you would be in the top 0.5% of people in the world! Podcasts and audiobooks are a uniquely versatile option for a busy schedule. Set up one to play in the background as you drive or with headphones as you complete household tasks. These can be an excellent way to gain knowledge but also a great way to distract you from what could be mundane tasks. If you typically have the TV running, shut it off and replace it with a podcast or audiobook. An extra two hours of informational content rather than junk television can put you miles ahead in your development and your ability to pass that knowledge on to others.

Learning new information and investing in yourself provides an automatic and natural reward to your system. Rewards should be part of any goal-setting system, but they are especially useful in helping your body acclimate itself to learning new information. James Clear, in his book Atomic Habits, explains; "your sensory nervous system is continuously monitoring which actions satisfy your desires and deliver pleasure. Feelings of pleasure and disappointment are part of the feedback mechanism that helps your brain distinguish useful actions from useless ones". Self-improvement provides your body with these feelings of pleasure and satisfaction naturally because you know you are making yourself into a better person and a more efficient worker. Pride and enjoyment in your work follow naturally. This makes the natural celebration your brain does after finishing a book or podcast episode much more fulfilling than eating a slice of chocolate cake to celebrate and regretting the excess sugar the next day. When you put in the work to improve yourself, you will have no regrets about the time spent pursuing such an important outcome.

The information you can learn if you take the time to do so can be invaluable, so try to set aside even a small amount of time each day to self-improvement. Spending just 30 minutes reading or listening in the morning equates to three hours a week. Adding this to your daily schedule will help to make reading a regular activity. Aim to read at least one book each month. You will be amazed at what you learn and what you can implement into your life when you are reading 12 books a year instead of one or less.

My Top 3 Podcast Recommendations:
1. **Addicted 2 Success** – Joel Brown
2. **The Ed Mylett Show** – Ed Mylett
3. **Success Talks**
4. **The Fizzle Show**
5. **Unstoppable** - Kerwin Rae

Chapter summary:

- Engaging in the right daily habits establishes a sturdy structure to build future successes
- Good habits help you improve yourself and get closer to your goals, while bad habits impede your progress
- Set new supportive habits and rid yourself of all of your bad habits through repetition of positive actions
- Figure out why you want to achieve your goals to give you the motivation to start new habits and get ahead of the competition
- Start small and build up to big changes
- Introduce new habits one at a time, and keep a tight schedule of your daily habits
- Exercise to provide yourself with a focus boost and shake off sleep
- Eating a healthy breakfast provides you with plenty of energy to get your day moving
- Visualize your goals each morning to help your subconscious mind
- Dedicate time to self-improvement by reading or listening to audiobooks and podcasts
- List the goals you need to get done at the start of every day

Step 4

The Goal Loop

The process of achieving your goals is less like a straight line and more like a circle. The goal loop makes use of the momentum you have built up over the course of achieving one goal to carry you through to starting on your next success. Once you achieve a goal, you have completed a loop, bringing you right back to the beginning of the circle to start on the next one. The daily habits, structures, systems and actions you have established during the first goal can be used to help you achieve future ones with some tweaking if necessary. Chaining your goals together in the goal loop gives you time to enjoy one success while making sure you do not delay starting on the next one. Make the best possible use of your time and energy by reinvesting it back into yourself and embarking on your next journey. I designed The Goal Loop to embody the idea of magnetic goals. Once you have completed one loop, it will be even easier to tackle others, and you will attract success to yourself now that you have learned the right way to tackle your goals.

The Phases of the Goal Loop

The Purpose of The Goal Loop

The goal loop provides a concrete, cyclical structure for all of your goal progress. It operates on the principles of rhythm, repetition, structure, clarity, and action. The phases allow you to develop a familiar rhythm of goal setting and achieving with positive feedback in the form of celebrating at the end. Because the phases loop back on themselves, they use repetition to encourage you to complete future goals. This process is similar to the repetition involved in daily habits which cause them to feel second nature after you have had enough practice incorporating them into your life. The goal loop is structured with an easy to follow path so you always know what the next step is, and there is no opportunity to waste precious time. It provides you with clarity on your next move and how to achieve what you have always wanted. Most important of all, it encourages perpetual action rather than stagnation. Once one goal is accomplished, it is time to move onto the next. If you keep moving, there is nothing you cannot achieve. The beauty of The Goal Loop is that each time you complete the cycle, your goal setting structure and systems gain strength and become extremely robust.

Cyclical Phases

The goal loop is broken up into four phases, each of which reflects a previously discussed aspect of the goal setting and achieving process.

Phase One is establishing your goals. Use this time to understand what you want to accomplish. *Phase Two* is the development of supportive daily habits that will help you get where you want to go. In *Phase Three*, you will take daily actions that propel you towards success. These phases culminate in achieving your goals, celebrating, and starting the goal loop anew armed with the knowledge you have learned from your last cycle.

Phase One: Setting Your Goals

Goal setting is the foundation of every cycle of goal achievement. Each time you return to the goal-setting phase, consider what you have learned from the last cycle. What goals worked for you? Which ones were easy to stick to, and which ones did you have a harder time finding the right motivation for? Are the goals you are setting in this cycle helping you to reach your 12-month goals, or have your 12-month goals changed? You should also be re-examining your *why factor* in this phase and making sure you still feel dedicated to the goals you set. Coming up with a powerful, solid set of goals that you feel passionately about in Phase One lays the foundation for the next phases and paves the way for future successes.

Phase Two: Supportive Daily Habits

You already know the amazing benefits that the right habits can have on your ability to achieve your goals. Knowing what works for you and what doesn't can help you revise and review your list of habits and identify which habits you can continue including in your schedule and which need to change. Update any habits that are specific to goals that have already been achieved to reflect your new ones. For example, if you have accomplished your first goal of weight loss and your new goal is developing muscle tone, you may need to establish a new workout routine to achieve different results. When reviewing your already existing daily habits and creating new ones, ask yourself the following questions. How is this habit helping me to achieve my current goals? Is there any new information I should direct my focus to learning? What habits were hardest to stick to last time, and why? How can I either modify these habits to make them more suited to my lifestyle and enjoyable? Answering these questions can help you keep your daily habits aligned as closely as possible to your goals.

Phase Three: Daily Action

Phase Three is about acting on the goals you have set and the habits you have chosen and taking actions every day that move you closer to the finish line. Many of the actions you take for various goals may be the same with only slight differences. For example, whether you are looking to start a new business or write a book, you will need to do research; however, the type of research you will have to do to successfully launch your business is different from the information you will have to gather for your book. You can use the actions you have completed for past goals to form a blueprint for your current ones and make the appropriate modifications when necessary. Remember to start with small actions and build up to larger ones, but keep moving forward no matter what. Daily actions help you build momentum that will carry you through to current and future goals.

Phase Four: Achieving Your Goals and Celebrating

You've done it! You have remained committed and focused, and in exchange, you have done what you have set out to do. Completing your goals can help you to feel more fulfilled on top of the benefits they already provide. The gratification from knowing your time and energy has paid off is immense. Take some time to appreciate all the hard work you have put into your success. Do something to celebrate, as you should be proud of yourself. Next, it is time to roll all of these positive feelings into motivation to tackle your next goal. You are likely riding high on positive emotions, and by now, you have realized the extent of what you are capable of. Success is a very powerful motivator. Armed with the knowledge and the proof that when you truly apply yourself, you really can accomplish what once felt like a faraway dream, starting on your next dream is the natural next step. Turn this success into achieving another goal, and another, until you are working your way up to your big 3-year and 5-year goals. You already have the tools and experience to ensure you are successful; you just need to put them to use by returning to the goal-setting loop. Decision Making with the Future in Mind

Following the path of The Goal Loop encourages you to think about your upcoming goals and your ideal future. It is a tool you can use to develop a plan that works for you and is unique to what you want to achieve while still being versatile enough to accommodate all of your goals. This means the decisions you make must also be forward-thinking as you consider what impact your choices have on your future.

Start establishing the goals you want to achieve as early as possible so you have every possible opportunity to establish positive habits and guide your decisions in the areas you choose to focus on. If you understand the relationship between your choices, the goal loop, and the end result of your life, you can use critical turning point moments and crucial decisions to effectively alter your future.

"We don't remember days; we remember moments."
Cesare Pavese (1908-1950)

Chapter summary:

- The goal loop is a circular pathway for inspiring consistent and repeated success
- Phase One of the goal loop involves goal setting and adjusting
- Phase Two is the development of useful habits you repeat each day to get closer to your goals
- Phase Three involves taking action and putting all of your plans into motion
- In Phase Four, celebrate the fruits of your efforts and use the morale boost to enter right back into phase one with new and improved goals
- The goal loop allows you to carry your momentum from one goal onto the next and repeat this process as often as necessary with regular reviews
- Make your decisions on this path with your ultimate future goals in mind. Only you can determine whether or not you succeed
- Looping your goals helps to minimize wasted time and get you going where you need to be

Step 5

The Key Pillars to Goal Achievement

Developing a healthy and productive mindset is imperative to goal success. Uncertainty and hesitation can keep you from making the most of every opportunity and can cause you to give up when you encounter difficulties. With a good mindset, you can overcome any obstacle and utilize every opportunity that comes your way, improving your chances of success. To win at the game of life, you absolutely must have a mindset that keeps you moving forward no matter the circumstances.

There are 10 key pillars that have provided huge success to me personally along with my clients that will give you the ability to achieve and maintain a healthy mindset. Each one flows into the next, and including all 10 in your daily habits is crucial. They complement each other, and when combined, they can give your productivity and forward momentum a significant turbo boost. To achieve your goals, incorporate each of these pillars as often as you can in your everyday practices. They will form the basic structure of your new productive mindset.

ONE

Set Your Goals

Having clearly defined goals gives you the mindset of an ambitious forward thinker. You are always considering your next move, getting ready to take your next step, and listening to the world around you with a discerning ear in search of any new opportunity. Goal setting opens you up to a whole new world of possibilities that might have otherwise gone unnoticed, and as a result, it works miracles for your mindset. You begin to look to the future rather than dwell in the past. You stop overthinking and start doing and plant your dreams into your subconscious mind.

Setting goals also makes it easier to kick negative

influences to the curb. Whether it is your own bad habits of self-doubt and worrying or the influence of others who do not value your goal as much as you do, freeing yourself of bad influences will improve your mindset and help you regain lost productivity. Even negative results will no longer have the power to hold you back because you know that the next big success is right around the corner. Brush aside anything that seeks to break your stride and always keep moving forward.

Setting Yourself Up for Success

Proper planning goes a long way in setting you up to succeed. Without the roadmap that setting your goals provides, it is hard to know where to go or what to do next. Having a proper plan that is clearly laid out for you allows you to proceed with confidence, knowing that your actions are bringing you closer to your goals. This is why goal setting is so important and forms the basis of any healthy mindset. Clear goals make it easy to understand what motivates you and the reasons you have for pushing forward. Without fully understanding your "why," your success mindset may falter when it encounters reasons for procrastination and waning interest. Knowing your goals and knowing why they matter to you sets you up to succeed in the remaining nine pillars of goal achievement.

TWO

Healthy Diet, Daily Exercise and the Right Amount of Sleep

Your physical health ties directly into your mental health and subsequently, your emotional state. If you keep your body in peak physical performance, it will repay you many times over with mental clarity. This means you should spend time taking care of your body in a variety of ways. Eating right, getting exercise, and allowing yourself enough time for sleep will improve your ability to focus and give you the energy you need to complete the tasks ahead of you. Your diet provides you with fuel for your body so you do not grow physically and mentally exhausted from eating irregularly or eating junk food. Exercise builds strength across your entire body, from your heart to your lungs to your brain. Sleep allows your body to rejuvenate itself from a hard day's work and prepare for the challenges of a brand-new day. Each of these areas is linked with the others, so faltering in even one area of the three can impact your overall efficiency. Prioritize your health, even if it means you have to occasionally readjust your deadlines; excessive stress can be dangerous, and without good health, you may not be able to see your goals through to the end or enjoy the fruits of your labor.

Improving Your Diet

Your diet affects your energy levels. It can be the determining factor in whether you are able to get done all you need to do. Not providing your body with enough fuel will lead to lower energy levels and distraction as your hunger can impede upon your thoughts. Similarly, filling up with junk food can leave you just as exhausted as your body is not getting the nutrients it craves for peak performance. Eating the right kinds of food in the right amounts benefits both your physical and mental health, which in turn allows you to take full advantage of those benefits when working towards your goals. A healthy body is the best way to ensure you have the energy you need to improve the other areas of your life.

Staying Fit

Physical exercise is one of the most important things you can do to boost your energy and keep yourself focused. Aim for around 30 minutes of exercise each day as a minimum, whether all at once or during short breaks interspersed with your work. Regular physical activity also provides long-term health benefits that help you reduce your risk of cardio-vascular disease, lower your blood cholesterol levels, lower the risk of type 2 diabetes, increase bone density, muscle strength and improve your overall health. Keeping yourself healthy gives you more time to work towards your goals without worrying about the health risks associated with a more sedentary lifestyle.

Even if you are not big on exercise, a short burst of jumping jacks or a quick walk can de-fog your head and get you back on the right track. Simply taking the stairs instead of the elevator whenever possible can give you a quick burst of endorphins that help you keep a positive focus on the task at hand. Physical activity stimulates various brain chemicals that may leave you feeling happier, more relaxed and less anxious. This improved mood does wonders for establishing a productive mindset, keeping you on the right track with just a quick exercise break.

Getting Adequate Sleep

Sleep allows your body to recover from the last day and prepare itself for a new day. Getting too little sleep can severely impede your ability to function at your best, leaving you trying to make up for the grogginess by supplementing it with caffeine. Getting a full night's rest helps you avoid caffeine crashes and wake up ready to tackle whatever the day's challenges are. Still, be sure not to spend too much time sleeping either. Oversleeping can also leave you feeling disoriented, and worse, it cuts into the time you have each day to accomplish your goals. Finding a happy medium between the two extremes will give you sufficient energy to accomplish everything you need to each day without lingering drowsiness. I personally aim for 7 hours sleep however you should be guided by your own body and be intuitive to when you need more sleep.

THREE

Supportive Daily Habits

As discussed at length in Step 3, your daily habits form the foundational structure of a productive day of work. They are the systems you follow to ensure you are always doing something to get closer to completing your goals. Habits are such an essential part of your life that they are considered character-defining. "What you repeatedly do (i.e., what you spend time thinking about and doing each day) ultimately forms the person you are, the things you believe, and the personality you portray" (James Clear, Atomic Habits). Therefore, your habits help to establish your mindset and determine what kind of a person you are.

Poor habits can lead you away from success, while positive ones help to make your dreams a reality. Daily habits for goal setting are good practices and positive actions that help you build up to greater successes. Use them to construct a daily routine that guides your actions and practices each day. Daily routines can help you establish priorities, limit procrastination, keep track of goals, and even make you healthier. They make action the default state rather than stagnation. Before you know it, you will be engaging in positive behaviors as automatically as you brush your teeth because they will just be routine parts of your day. If you set good habits rather than ones that encourage hesitancy and wasting time, you will further develop your success mindset and help keep yourself productive.

Examples of Daily Habits

The types of daily habits most beneficial to you will depend on exactly what your goals are. If your goal is to travel more or to visit a specific destination, you will have more luck with daily habits that involve automation of your finances or saving money for your trip. If your goal is to get fit and lose weight, your daily habits might include looking up new healthy recipes and trying something new. Make sure your habits are specific to the goal you are trying to achieve and that they are repeatable actions you can complete every day. Some examples of daily habits include:

- 30 minutes of daily exercise
- A brief meditation or visualization exercise
- Eating a nutritious breakfast each day
- Keeping a journal and writing down one or two things you are grateful for each day
- Writing your top 10 goals and your top three priorities for the day
- Numbering your daily tasks in order of importance
- At the end of each day, recording the tasks and priority actions for tomorrow

FOUR

Gratitude

It may seem somewhat counterintuitive at first, but being grateful for what you do have is a great way to encourage yourself to pursue new goals. Gratification greatly benefits your mindset and has been proven to boost your fulfillment in life. A recent study that was reported by Happy Living in 2019 had different groups write down positive or negative events every day. Those in the grateful group experienced less reported levels of depression and stress, exercised more regularly, made greater progress toward achieving personal goals and were more likely to help others in need, proving that simply being grateful can completely change your outlook. Additionally, those that practice gratitude are more creative, bounce back more quickly from adversity and have stronger social relationships than those who don't. Gratitude helps you overcome challenges and work around problems because you know that you have a great deal to be proud of in your life already.

How to Increase Your Gratitude

Increasing your gratitude is an exercise in balance. A daily gratification process helps you recognize the great things you already have in life while also maintaining your interest in achieving more. Thinking you have everything can make you complacent in your current state, but thinking you have nothing can make further achievements feel impossible. Therefore, you must set a baseline of gratefulness upon which you build your success mindset.

In order to boost your gratitude, start by writing

one or two things down every day that you are thankful for. These can be reflections on your past and how far you have come, current events, travel and life experiences, family and friends, achievements you have earned, opportunities you have taken advantage of, or anything else you are grateful for. Make this practice an everyday activity. Taking time each day to reflect on the things in your life that matter to you will give you the confidence to make new leaps and bounds and the mindset to appreciate each new opportunity. Gratefulness puts you in a mindset that makes you open to receiving whatever the universe throws at you next, good or bad, which in turn encourages you to give back whenever possible.

FIVE

Love and Appreciation for Your Friends, Family, and Community

There are many things in life that you can live without. You can skip out on that bag of chips in between meals. You can avoid buying that pair of shoes you've had your eye on, or you can miss out on the release of a new movie because you are too busy. Inadvisable as it may be, you can skip a few hours of sleep when required. But one thing you absolutely cannot live without is love. To be able to love and be loved is ingrained in our DNA. Our friends, families, and communities are essential parts of our lives and make us who we are. Keep your loved ones close and do not forget the support they have provided you, and you have provided them in turn.

The Importance of Relationships

Many people sacrifice their relationships in their pursuit of financial wealth and success. They allow friendships to deteriorate and neglect family ties as they pour more and more time into their work. It is the type of single-minded determination that may beef up your bank account but at the expense of what really matters. You can have all the money in the world, but if you neglect your relationships with others, you will reach the peak of the mountain, turn around, and realize you have no one to share it with. The love of those we care about is what makes the whole journey worthwhile. Without it, all the work you put towards your goal will feel meaningless.

Make time for your friends, family, and community members. If they help you along your path to success, support them in kind. At the end of your life, you will not care about how much money you have in your bank account because as the old adage goes, you can't take it with you! Instead, you will look back on your life and fondly remember the people you've met, the relationships you've forged, the places you've visited, your shared laughter, and the positive impact you've had on other people.

SIX

Dealing with Challenges and Sacrifices

Throughout life, we experience plenty of challenges we must navigate. Your ability to appropriately react to these difficulties is closely connected to your mindset, and we all respond to them differently. Some people remain calm and think through all options. Others hit the panic button right away and are more likely to curl up in the foetal position than they are to reason their way through a problem, at least at first. Still, others start out calm but rapidly dissolve into fear and doubt from overthinking and ceaseless worrying. There are also those who simply shut down, treating any roadblock like a complete failure. While there's a myriad of poor ways to react to complications, you will generally get more out of keeping cool under stress than you will by flying into a blind panic. But if your default response is less ideal, how do you learn how to keep a level head?

Whatever challenge, event, or incident you are thrown, you have the choice of how to react. Our default reactions are typically based on our past experiences, which may involve childhood encounters with the same or similar situations, or we may simply follow in the footsteps of our parents and deal with difficulties the same way they did. However, the way our ingrained responses are may not always be the most appropriate, especially if we are simply repeating the mistakes of the past. Stop, and take a moment to breathe and think through the realistic results of the setback and the most likely outcome. From there, you can begin to brainstorm possible ways of overcoming the problem and getting yourself back on track. You can recover from setbacks with the right mindset, so develop your resilience to become stronger from each knock you receive.

Surmounting Challenges

When dealing with challenges, the most successful leaders respond calmly and methodically to high-pressure situations. They keep everyone around them calm and take the lead in difficult times. The best leaders take in all available information, assess the situation, and use their experience to make a decision that is in the best interests of everyone they are responsible for. Emulate them the best you can and try not to leap to any hasty decisions. Take time to come up with a thoughtful response that is likely to work rather than throwing everything at the wall and seeing what sticks. When the stock market dips, you do not want to be one of the people selling for pennies because you panicked and decided you had to cut your losses, especially if the same stock rises the next day again. Take the time to get as much information about the situation as you can before you decide if it is better to hang in there or change your course.

It is imperative to take responsibility for your choices in these situations and recognize that we are in control of how we deal with our emotions. By keeping calm and reassessing the situation, you can flip a negative situation into a beneficial one. Listen to the challenges the universe is testing you with and use them as learning opportunities rather than stumbling blocks. They may not appear to be good things at the time, but consider your history of encountering challenges and what came out of them. The vast majority of the time, you have learned a valuable lesson or changed your life's course for the better. You wouldn't be where you are today without the adversity you have faced, so don't shy away from it when it occurs.

Making Sacrifices

What would you sacrifice to live your dream life? Would you get up an hour earlier, or work a few hours later on a Friday rather than surfing the web? Would you purchase a second-hand car to save money rather than wasting savings on a flashy new car you only bought to impress people whose opinions really don't matter? If you're not prepared to make sacrifices when they count, you cannot expect to have your dream handed to you. This is why it is so important to care deeply about your goals instead of following the path someone else has laid out for you. If your goals are really what you want, you will have no problem skipping unnecessary luxuries or working a little harder, and as a result, there should be no questioning your ability to succeed. Choosing to give up excess comforts isn't always the easiest one, but it is the one that's guaranteed to bring you closer to your goals.

Still, there are healthy ways to make sacrifices and unhealthy ones. Deciding to skip fast food for weight loss, or giving up the reliability of a steady income in favor of starting a business, are reasonable sacrifices with a high potential for positive results. Cutting out family time and losing track of your relationships with friends and family, on the other hand, is an unhealthy sacrifice that can impede upon your success and happiness in the long run. Be sure you are not giving up the things that really matter in life just to push the deadline for success a little closer; reaching your goals is ideal, but there is no point if you end up with no one to share it with or sacrifice your health and well-being to get there.

The extent of sacrifice you are prepared to make is entirely up to you. You may be willing to take the plunge and entirely alter your life to conquer a challenge and meet your goals, or you may prefer a more long-term method of slow and consistent changes that build up into a bigger sacrifice. How drastic a change is needed is dependent on how much time you have allowed yourself to achieve your goal and how big of a goal it is. Knowing what will be required for a big goal isn't always apparent at the beginning of the journey, but you will quickly learn that all goals require commitment and some level of sacrifice. Only you can decide what price you are willing to pay to achieve your dreams.

SEVEN

Positively Impact Others

Meeting your goals is not just about helping yourself; it is also about helping others. Providing support to those around you is a win-win situation for all involved. They receive whatever help you can provide them, and you receive the knowledge that you have made a positive impact on someone's life, as well as improving your relationship with that person. They may even remember what you have done for them and make efforts to repay you in the future. This is commonly known as 'Paying it forward'. This sets up a cycle of positivity that ultimately makes your community a better place to live.

How to Help

We are all granted opportunities to affect others' lives. You may help those around you as a teacher, a volunteer, a parent, a brother or sister, an uncle or aunt, a role model, a manager, or in many, many other ways. To be a positive influence for someone else is a great gift, whether you affect the lives of millions or just one person. Some believe they have nothing to give or teach others, but the small things can be just as valuable. You could assist someone struggling with their luggage on a plane, hold the door for the person behind you, or even provide some basic science tutoring for a family friend. These are things that cost you very little but could mean the world to someone else. If you are still in doubt, you can also make an effort to be encouraging to those around you. When we see the value and potential in others and then convey to them what we see, we are making a positive impact. Showing others how to recognize their value, or simply saying you appreciate the work someone is doing, is a great way to lift their spirits and make your own mindset more appreciative of those around you. A little positivity goes a long way in making the world a better place. If you get a reputation for being kind and appreciative, others will likely treat you with the same courtesy.

"You can get everything in life you want if you will just help enough other people to get what they want."
Zig Ziglar (1926-2012)

Be Kind to Others

Treating others kindly is a key pillar of real success. Indeed, you could become successful by stepping over others and disregarding their wishes at every turn. But what kind of success would that be? Earning goals through dishonesty and leaving behind a trail of dissatisfied customers and disgruntled strangers is no real success. We have all heard stories of celebrities that have mistreated and disappointed fans, or CEOs accused of presenting others' ideas as their own. These stories can sour listeners and, in some cases, even affect the ability of those involved in them to be successful. You can avoid a similar fate by remaining kind and spreading that kindness as best as you can. It takes minimal effort to be a positive force in the world rather than a negative one.

Being kind to others involves following two elementary key values. The first is treating everyone with respect, kindness, and love. Even complete strangers should be approached starting from a basis of respect. You never know who is going to become important in your life in the future, and even if you never see someone again after your first meeting, you are still leaving a positive impression on them. Treating everyone with basic decency goes a long way towards receiving respect in return and helps improve everyone's daily experiences. The second key value is treating people how you would like to be treated yourself. More often than not, others' behaviors towards you will mirror your behavior towards them. We get out of this world what we put into it; if you want to receive good things, then you have to put those good things out into the world yourself.

The Golden Rule

There is a reason why treating others as you want to be treated is so prevalent in otherwise highly dissimilar cultures to the point that it is referred to as the golden rule. It is found in many major world religions and the personal philosophies of many successful people. The way you interact with those around you is a mark of the legacy you leave on the world. How you treat others is a direct reflection of you. You may claim to be a moral person who acts fairly, but your actions need to match this claim. Do you demonstrate integrity? Are you polite? Do you make sure you keep your promises? Would you help a stranger who needed it? If you would hope someone would help you in the same situation, then you should practice the same kindness for everyone else.

Many situations can be improved by being kind to others, even if they are not kind to you. In these cases, maintaining civility and respect is almost always better than devolving into anger and insults, and often causes the aggravated party to reconsider their own stance more effectively than belligerent arguing.

Being kind is not just good for others; it is also good for you. There are many mental health benefits associated with practicing kindness. You may have noticed that after losing your patience and snapping at someone, you have felt regretful and disappointed in yourself. This is because the act of being unkind fosters negative thoughts and increases your blood pressure and your fatigue. It can also cause interruptions to your sleep, can distract you from important and enjoyable activities and even impact other relationships. To the contrary, kindness has been linked to improving your mood, lowering your blood pressure and increasing your positive thinking. There are many altruistic reasons to be kind. Still, there is no shortage of "selfish" reasons either, and nothing is preventing you from taking advantage of the positive effects while still putting good energy out into the world.

EIGHT

The Confidence Factor

Low self-esteem can occur at a startlingly young age. Though we all start out ready to take on the world, doubts about what we are really capable of begin to creep up on us as we grow older and are taught that our dreams are unrealistic. Our self-esteem, accordingly, takes a hit. One study of American youths found that at four years old, 96% of study participants had high self-esteem and a good self-image, but by the time they reached 18, fewer than 5% maintained this positive self-image. We are encouraged to look at our capabilities realistically, even as we are told to follow our dreams. The result is adults with low self-esteem that do not believe themselves capable of accomplishing their dreams.

"The happiness of your life depends upon the quality of your thoughts." Marcus Antonius (86-161 AD)

Low self-esteem also tends to compound itself the longer it is allowed to remain as part of your psyche. If you already feel negative about yourself, you will look for examples that prove it to be true, even while ignoring any that suggest the opposite. You engage in a sort of unconscious confirmation bias, in which all new experiences seem to prove that you are not good enough to achieve anything else. You are blinded to the times when you performed very well at a task, and you restrict yourself from leaving your comfort zone, even if it might mean discovering something new that you are good at. The way to break this cycle of uncertainty and doubt is to improve your self-esteem. Your thoughts have a direct impact on your happiness, and it is only by recognizing that you are, in fact, capable of amazing things that you can defeat lingering doubts.

Ditching Limiting Beliefs

Once you begin to take charge of your self-esteem, you can cut the cord with limiting beliefs for good. Keeping your negative beliefs around will ultimately cause you to play it safe when you should be taking risks. As a Forbes magazine article points out, "Deep down we know we are here to shine and play big. But the stories we tell ourselves mean we hold back through fear. We play it safe. We end up living only half a life" (Burnford, 2019, para. 8). Allowing limiting beliefs to maintain control over your life means you will never be able to live freely and experience everything you should be able to do. If you never take a chance, you will never know just what you could have accomplished.

Learn to sort through your beliefs and identify which ones are limiting you. Embrace the beliefs that allow you to achieve more and go further, and ditch those that leave you living "only half a life." If you have been preventing yourself from trying something new because you already decided you won't be any good at it, you must leave these preconceived notions behind and embrace the idea that you can't know how good you are at something until you give it a shot. Reflect on all the times you did very well rather than ruminating on any mistakes or slip-ups. Commend yourself every time you get back up and try again after what feels like a defeat. Before you know it, you will be tackling obstacles with self-assurance you didn't think you were capable of. A lack of confidence has no place in a successful life, so it should have no place in your life.

If you were to become truly successful, what would you need to do differently? What actions do you take that are informed by limiting beliefs, and which ones have you avoided for the same reasons? Answering these questions can help you realize the importance of thinking positively and disregarding the ideas you have about yourself and your limitations that will only ever hold you back.

Overcoming Challenges and Setbacks

We all face different challenges that can get in the way of accomplishing our goals. Whether they come in the form of a minor inconvenience or a life-altering moment, unexpected circumstances can trip us up when we are just beginning to pick up momentum. While it is impossible to avoid setbacks entirely, that does not mean that you have to allow them to control your ability to achieve your goals. No matter what your personal challenges are, facing them with the right attitude and remaining persistent in the face of doubt will carry you through to success.

Managing Setbacks

From this moment onward, make your philosophy a commitment to never giving up. If you allow hardships to discourage you, you risk passing up future opportunities and missing out on your goals. This can snowball into complete stagnation. Neglecting to develop this mindset will end up destroying your confidence and ability to believe in yourself, which spells disaster for your chances at success. No matter what difficulties you encounter, you must be willing to keep moving forward and trying again. Manage rejection by pressing onwards and don't let anything keep you down. Still, this does not mean that you need to keep pursuing something the same way if it has not been working for you so far. Use failures as a way to gauge what works and what doesn't, and shape your future attempts accordingly until you find the right recipe for success. Melanie Perkins, a technology entrepreneur, faced over a hundred rejections before she finally found success, but the rejections were not wasted efforts. She "revised [her] pitch deck again and again until it was strong enough to find the right partners," and found that "the experiences we value most in life are often the most challenging. They push you out of your comfort zone and help you grow" (The Oracles, 2018). Without the right mindset and the courage to keep revising her pitch, Perkins may not have found the success she did. Your personal philosophy is an essential tool you have in achieving your goals.

Failure can be difficult to accept, but even the most successful people have had to experience failure at one time or another. The best way to view these temporary setbacks is to view them not as causes of misfortune but as opportunities to learn and grow. Every failure has something to teach us, and every hardship imparts a lesson when we can overcome it, even if that lesson is as simple as the power of never giving up. Additionally, many failures can be circumnavigated simply by stepping back and changing your perspective. This sense of perspective will help you step away from the 'noise without giving up on your goal, instead leaving you viewing it from numerous vantage points while considering other options. Your newfound perspective will then allow you to reconsider the severity of the failure and discover a solution with a clear and calm mind.

Unnecessary Worry

In life, there will simply be some things that are forever out of your control. As much as you may wish to have some influence over these things so that you can use them to your advantage, it is impossible to do so. Learning to accept and expect this is part of any healthy outlook for facing challenges. Aspects of daily life like the actions of other people and overly negative co-workers are not under your control, and neither are the weather or the stock market. Instead of seeking to control these parts of life or constantly worrying about them, you should do your best to manage your reactions to them. You can see a rainy day as a delay in the yard work you were going to get done, or you can see it as a perfect opportunity to fix those small ceiling cracks that have been bothering you for weeks. You cannot control everything, but you can minimize the negative impact you allow unfortunate circumstances to have on your life.

NINE
Invest in Yourself and Your Wealth

You must invest time and energy into yourself in order to see results. There is a famous saying that says 'the more you learn, the more you earn'. This is absolutely true when it comes to goal setting. You must improve yourself to improve your wealth and your quality of work. This means taking every opportunity to learn and grow. Making investments in yourself in the form of knowledge and experiences will significantly increase your value, not to mention helping you lead a more personally fulfilling life. Research performed by the University of Calgary indicated that consistently working the evaluative aspects of your brain and challenging yourself to learn more leads to far greater happiness and fulfillment than using your free time for passive activities like watching TV. Using available time to improve yourself rather than catching up on the latest pop culture fad is a much better use of your time and resources. Investments can come in a variety of forms and from a variety of sources, so always keep an eye and an ear out for new ways to improve yourself.

Sources for Improvement

These days, the resources to improve ourselves are closer than ever before. The practices and thought processes of the highly successful are readily available across the internet, in print, and in person. Make use of these various pathways as often as you can. Read an article written by someone successful in the same area as your goals, or attend a seminar on how to get ahead. Pick up a book or audiobook written by someone who knows what they're talking about. For only a few dollars, you can get information worth its weight in gold without even leaving the house. This is the very definition of investing in yourself. If you want to make a change, try the following experiment. Stop listening to music, local radio, and even news in the car. Instead, use that time to listen to an enlightening podcast or audiobook. If you commute for an average of eight hours a week, you could be gaining 32 hours of education each month that you would have otherwise spent listening to the same negative news stories or repetitive songs. If you commit to using your idle time to improve yourself for just one month, you will realize how much time you would otherwise waste each day and never want to go back.

TEN
Make Each Day Count

Many feel that old age is a very distant worry that they do not need to concern themselves with now. However, the time you have left grows shorter every day, which is all the more reason to take advantage of the time you have now rather than letting it slip through your fingers. None of us can give ourselves more time, no matter how much money we have. There are only 24 hours, just 1,440 minutes, in each day. What you do with these 1,440 minutes will define the experiences you have, the success you generate, and who you are. When you are 85 years old and looking back at your life, you want to be proud of all you have accomplished, not regretful you did not make the most of the days you had.

Making each day count is a time management game. Learning to make the best possible use of your time is an invaluable tool for achieving your goals and maintaining a productive and success-driven mindset. Try to deal with the most important things first, learn to say no to low priority or unnecessary activities and plan your day so that you always know what is next. Additionally, keep your energy levels in mind during your planning to avoid exhausting yourself. You can have every minute of the day packed with essential tasks, but if you don't have the energy to complete them properly, then it's all for nothing. Overexerting yourself can be just as dangerous to your productivity and output quality as putting off work, so manage your time in a way that allows for a good balance between action and rest.

Adding More Working Years

While none of us can turn back time (even Cher made a song about it in the 90's!), good time management allows you to effectively expand the time in your schedule by as much as years. If you decide to get up at 5:30 am rather than 7:30 am for five days a week, you would end up with 10 extra hours you can put to good use each week. Those extra 10 hours become 40 hours a month, and a year of following this practice is 480 extra hours. This is an additional 13 weeks' worth of 40-hour work weeks of improvement and self-investment each year. If you start waking earlier at 40 and continue until you turn 65, you will invest over six additional years' worth of time into your goals.

Following this simple practice adds years of development and knowledge. All it takes is some discipline and commitment. If you genuinely want to do more, be more, and achieve more, you must make use of the time you have. Making this investment benefits not just you but also others who can benefit from all of the knowledge you have accrued. Living each day to its fullest and packing in as much growth as possible will take you to new heights and bring your chances of success way above those of your competitors as you experience firsthand the value of hard work and determination.

Chapter summary:

- A success-oriented mindset will propel you towards your goals
- 10 pillars make up the foundation of your success mindset
- Clearly define your goals and understand why they matter to you
- Improve your physical health through diet, exercise, and sleep to improve your daily output
- Develop a robust system of supportive daily habits that feed into your goals
- Be grateful for all the good things you have in your life
- Appreciate your friends, family, and community
- Know the sacrifices you are willing to make to conquer challenges in the way of your goals
- Do your best to help others and make a positive impact on your community
- Have a positive and kind attitude towards those around you

Step 6

The Fear Thermometer

The thermometer of fear is very different for each of us. What is feared by one person to the extent that it stops them in their tracks is happily accommodated by another, and barely registers as a concern to others. This is because our fears are learned. They can come from our past negative experiences or be taught to us by the experiences and fears of those we come into contact with, but they are not inherent to everyone. This means, of course, that fears can be unlearned just as they can be learned. This can provide its own unique set of challenges; still, we must push back against what holds us back in order to make any real progress.

One product of fear is the limiting beliefs that we hold about ourselves. Fear can be introduced at any stage of our life, but our limiting beliefs are usually a direct result of something that has occurred to us in childhood. They convince us that we are not good at certain activities, sometimes those that we have not even tried, and make us too afraid to try because we might fail. Being unable to branch out and take risks because of your limiting beliefs can get in the way of your success, leaving you worrying about the risk of failure. But why are we so afraid of failure? Yes, it means that our efforts were not successful, but failure rarely means we have wasted our time or efforts. Failure is, at its worst, merely a temporary setback, so why is it such a powerful anti-motivator in our lives?

The fear of failure holds us back and keeps us from trying new things. Learning to conquer your fear of failing and instead embracing the idea of failure will give you the confidence to push the boundaries and leave your comfort zone far behind. Failure is never a complete loss; it is a learning experience that teaches you what worked, what didn't, and what you should do next time to avoid a similar result. It is always better than never trying at all. Additionally, every time you experience failure and overcome it, your fear of failure will decrease. You will learn that failing is not so bad after all, which gives you a great deal of freedom and encourages experimentation. If you persevere and don't let failure stop you, you will eventually reach success no matter how many times you fail. To succeed, you need to learn to embrace failure.

Don't Quit – Pivot and Change Direction

How do you know when it's time to quit? Every time you experience a major setback, you have likely considered throwing your hands up and yelling these two little words – "I quit!" It is all too easy to quit; it is much harder to keep going. When in doubt, return to your '*why*' factor. Why are you doing this? Why are you trying to get out of it, and is it worth trying again? If I was to push on and it did work out, what would I gain? What are the consequences if I don't take this leap forward? If you do not care about what you are trying to achieve, such as working in a job you hate or trying to learn something you have no passion for, it may be time to go back to the drawing board, pivot and then figure out what your new goals should be. If you are truly dedicated to your goals, the reasons for trying again will be abundant. You will find the resolve to take the road less travelled rather than the easy way out of quitting. Armed with your why factor, giving up no longer seems like such an appealing idea!

Utilizing your why factor in this way helps you flirt with danger. You may be uneasy with failure, but that doesn't always have to be a bad thing if you are ready to put yourself out there for the right reasons and with the right mindset. Worrying that failure may occur, simply means you are doing something different that you cannot predict the outcome of. To achieve success, this is an absolute necessity. To overcome it, think about the potential positive outcomes rather than the negatives. If you are doing something that really matters, you can encourage yourself to push past your hesitation because you know the outcome is more important than the fear. If you know your success will help people and make your community a better place, then you will be more likely to keep pushing even when there is a possibility of failing. Your positive impact at the end of all of your attempts is important enough that you can't give up on them. If your decision is not to quit, then congratulations. You have just done what many others before you have failed to do. Remember, successful people are just those who get back up on off the canvas one more time than everyone else. Your ability to overcome setbacks will serve you well as you chase your goals. Now that quitting is no longer an option, it is time to re-examine your failure and find out how you can use it to help you instead. Embrace and learn from your failure. What did it teach you about potential pitfalls to avoid in future attempts? What worked, and what needs to be adjusted? Without failing, these are lessons you may never have learned.

Fighting Fear with Self-Confidence

Even if you learn to accept the possibility of failure, you may never be able to entirely rid yourself of your fear. You can take all the necessary steps to understand and appreciate the role of failure in your success story. Still, an undercurrent of fear is only natural when you are drastically shifting the course of your life and navigating uncharted waters. While you cannot completely control your fear, you can control how you choose to respond to it. Being afraid does not have to mean you shut down. You cannot control failure either, but you can control how you respond to it and to what extent you let the fear of failure dictate your life.

"It's not what you are dealt with in life; it's how you deal with it."
J.M Schofield

Start by becoming aware of what emotions you begin to feel so that you can identify them and change your response pattern. Take notice of the nervous, tingly feeling that precedes it and the way your body enters fight or flight mode when stressed. Fear increases the speed of your heartbeat and distorts your capacity for clear thinking, which can make decision making nearly impossible until you have calmed yourself. Once you have cognitively recognized the signs of fear, you can begin to utilize strategies for keeping a level head and returning to a calm and collected state. If you think of your fear and your body's response to that fear as a wall that limits your progress, you need to come up with a reliable way to conquer the wall.

One way to do so is by developing and reinforcing your self-confidence. If you are confident in yourself and your abilities, you will know that there is nothing that can stop you from achieving your goals, should you set your mind to it. Failure will no longer be a negative outcome worth worrying over. It will be just another test from the universe to determine if you are ready for success. Having high self-confidence means believing that yes, you are ready for success, and the current setback is not going to keep you down for long.

To minimize symptoms of fear, you can try to understand the source of your panic. Knowing what outcome you are most afraid of can help put your concerns into perspective, as the reality of the situation is often less drastic than the worst thing your mind can come up with. Once you have identified the cause of your anxieties, assist with a return to the gratefulness exercises you practiced earlier in step 2. Reflect on all the positive things you still have in your life, and your potential losses will not feel so big after all. Fighting your fears with self-confidence, gratitude, and a positive mindset helps to make them more manageable and less world-ending.

To get to the root cause of your fears and calm your worry, ask yourself the following questions:

- Is your fear a perceived fear of what might not even happen, rather than what most likely will occur?

- Does everyone else share your fear? If not, why not?

- Is there someone who doesn't share your fear? If so, have you talked to them about their reason for not sharing the same fear?

- What's the absolute worst thing that could happen if your fear became a reality? Would it be the end of the world?

- Are you making the fear bigger than what it really is?

- If you could overcome your fear, what success could you achieve? Is the fear so great that you would rather continue carrying it than overcoming it and achieving the success you've always wanted?

Turn your fear on its head. What are the consequences you will experience or the opportunities you may miss if you don't try the thing you are afraid of?

Answering these questions honestly will give you greater insight into how you deal with fear, how you can manage and overcome it in the future, and the limitations fear is having on your future success. These questions are not meant to invalidate your fears; instead, they will show you through your own reasoning that what once seemed terrifying was only a smaller problem blown out of proportion. Once you understand the real extent of the setback, you can begin moving past it.

Charge Ahead and Keep Falling Forward

Failure is a learning experience, so pay attention and make sure you make the most of every misstep. Each time we fail, we learn new information about our goal and how to get there.

You may stumble and fall, but you fall forward, equipped with the knowledge you've gained and ready to get back up, possibly fall again, and get up once more. This makes failing a more valuable experience than it initially seems. In truth, failure teaches us the hard lessons about persistence that we need to succeed. Persistence is a key factor that determines your chances of success, and to be persistent, you must first fail; otherwise, there is no need to persist. Learn to embrace failure – own it, learn from it and take full responsibility for making sure that mistake doesn't happen again. Many people avoid failure at all costs, even giving up progress on their goals to remove all chances of failure. But most fears, especially those surrounding failure, are based on imagined thoughts rather than facts. They hold us back from seeing the truth of the matter and keep us from charging ahead unless we know how to face them.

Facing your fears isn't easy no matter what you are afraid of. If you are claustrophobic, stepping into an elevator can feel like an insurmountable task. And if you fear challenges and failure, you can remain rooted in place. Each of these fears has the power to keep us immobile, but they are all products of our thoughts exaggerating possible consequences. It is unlikely that anything is hiding in the dark corners of your room other than your dresser, and it is similarly unlikely that our worst fears will come true after a failure. Learning to face your fears is like turning the lights on in that dark room to see that everything is exactly how you left it, and there is no reason to be afraid. If you recontextualize failure and begin to see it as an opportunity, not a roadblock, your fears surrounding it will melt away. Keep your eyes on the prize and keep your goals at the forefront of your mind rather than getting stuck on the problem. Conquering your fears is the first step to taking on risks that will benefit you in the long run.

Learning to Take Risks

There are so many opportunities at your fingertips if you can simply convince yourself to take the first step. Can you imagine if some of the world's best inventors, explorers, leaders, or writers were not prepared to take the first step? We would be missing so many of the things we take for granted today such as the light bulb, the smartphone, air travel, and the computer. Luckily, these great minds were prepared to take the appropriate risks, even if it meant they had to fail many times before they were successful. While it can be hard to open yourself to the idea of putting yourself out there, the success you are striving for depends on a heightened level of risk; therefore, failure is simply a common by-product. Without being willing to take risks, you will never be able to commit yourself to the first step, which means you will be unable to make meaningful progress.

With any new journey, there is going to be a point where all the planning is over, and it is time to take that first step into the unknown. It can be daunting, as all new ventures seem at first, but it can also be an opportunity to completely change your life for the better. Think about the times you have taken risks before, and the times they have worked out for you, and even the times they haven't ended as you wanted. How different would your life be without those defining moments? What would your life look like if you hadn't taken the first step? Alternatively, what could your life look like if you had taken an opportunity you let pass you by? It is not the steps you have taken that you will come to regret, but the ones you failed to take. Inaction has the power to haunt you with what-ifs for the rest of your life. Some people believe that your first step has to be a big risk, but that is untrue. Your first steps can start out small and slowly build over time to the more life-changing steps. Start small and work your way up. Taking your first step towards a personal goal, a new relationship, or starting a new business is often an opportunity to gain new information, experience, and skills. These experiences help you build momentum that makes tackling the big stuff much less scary.

Building Forward Momentum

Momentum is what keeps a moving object in motion. It can turn a single small act into a wide array of positive actions. To gain momentum, you need to make your first decision and take that first step; after that, the process will become easier so long as you stick with it. Think of it like trying to push a stationary car. The first ten steps are often the hardest, and you will need a significant amount of force to get things moving, but as the wheels start rolling and the car builds momentum, each step becomes easier. Before you know it, your steps become longer, the force you need to apply decreases, and you have made significant progress.

What you want to avoid is stagnation, or in other words, procrastination that interferes with your momentum and results in standing still. If you stopped halfway through pushing the stationary car, you would have to build up your starting momentum all over again. Every time you stop, you have to take that first difficult step again. Hesitation and doubt can be fatal for your momentum and keep you from building up speed, so don't allow instances of failure to halt your progress for longer than you need to decide how to proceed. Even making the wrong call is better than making no call at all because it allows you to keep your momentum, making it easier to course correct and fix what is wrong rather than giving up.

If you're not prepared to put in the work and energy necessary for momentum at the beginning, you will never reach the stage where momentum carries you further. Too many give up in the early stages because there are too many difficulties. If you simply proceed one step at a time, understanding that early challenges will lead to less work later on, you will be prepared to get through the toughest stage of your journey successfully. Take action, fall forward, and don't allow your limiting beliefs to pull the handbrake.

Chapter summary:

- To achieve great success, stop fearing failure
- Failure is a learning experience that will help you grow and teach you how to respond to roadblocks
- Overcome the reactive desire to quit by thinking about the good that trying again and succeeding will do
- To manage your fears, improve your self-confidence
- Question how realistic your fears are before you allow them to dominate your thoughts
- View failure as an opportunity, not a catastrophic outcome
- Learn what you can from every failure so that you can avoid falling into the same pitfalls
- You cannot fail if you never try, but you also cannot try and succeed unless you accept the risk of failure
- Start with small changes and build the necessary momentum to make bigger, more impactful decisions

Step 7

The Support Network

The final step in achieving your goals is developing a supportive network of great people. You deserve people who will stand in your corner, encourage you to keep going in the difficult times, cheer for you when you make progress, and celebrate like the clock has just struck midnight on New Year's when you succeed. Having the right people backing you can make or break your efforts to improve yourself and your life. Seek out people who genuinely care for you and want to see you succeed, and seriously reconsider being around those who don't want you to make any progress or consistently bring negativity into your life.

A strong support network can help you achieve a

variety of goals. They can help you find and acquire the resources you need to succeed, either through their connections or by helping you with research and information gathering. They can keep you motivated when the road ahead is uncertain so that you do not lose your forward momentum. They can help you recover and move forward after a failure. Perhaps most importantly, they can be a crutch to lean on for support when you face difficult situations. Whatever the hardship you are experiencing, the people in your support network will be there for you when you need a shoulder to lean on after a long day, or when you are feeling overwhelmed with work, school or a current setback. The moral support that a connected and robust network provides can be invaluable, especially when you genuinely care about the opinions of the people in your network. With the encouragement and understanding of friends, family, and colleagues at your side, success does not seem so far away after all.

Your Support Network

When determining who you will include in your support network, there are a few key factors to keep an eye out for. First, you are going to want to look for people that are interested in the area of your goals. Seek out those who have already achieved what you want or who are actively pursuing the same or similar things. These people will be able to empathize with the struggles unique to your goals, and they can often provide valuable advice for what to do next. There's no point in trying to blindly guess what to do if it's already been done before. Not only will you save valuable time and money by seeking out more knowledgeable people, but you also have the opportunity to expand on what they have accomplished and get even better results. Look for sources of good advice that can get you through tough decisions and guide your steps to success.

By developing connections and even friendships with high-level achievers, you will begin to get a sense of what it takes to get to their level. You will see the amount of work they put into achieving their goals and the rewards they have reaped from their continued dedication. Understanding what it takes to get to the next level involves asking smart questions that allow for informative, helpful answers. The best questions are specific about what you want to achieve and will enable the responder to elaborate if they choose. Avoid overly general questions like "how did you get so successful?" and instead try to be more precise with what you want to know. Keep an open mind and seriously consider any advice you are given, even if it is not the answer you were expecting. Great questions will draw out great answers which you can use for your growth and advancement.

Of course, not everyone in your support group is going to know more than you about your goals. Some members have the alternate but equally important role of providing moral support and encouragement. More often than not, this is where friends and family come in. If you are close to members of your family and you have friends that support you and want you to succeed, they also make excellent additions to your support network.

Building Your Team

Whoever you choose to allow into your support network, approach the process like you are conducting a job interview for potential employees of *Your Life, Inc.* This does not mean you have to sit members of your family down for formal interviews, but it does mean you should honestly and carefully consider who will allow you to achieve the most success. Not everyone in your life will be well suited to supporting you in your endeavors, so you must make smart and careful choices. Do your best to attract like-minded people that understand your goals and want to help you achieve them. Your support network will become your team of professional advisors and business partners that guide you to the right choices and help to keep Your Life, Inc. as successful as possible.

Qualities to Look for

How do you know if someone would be a good member of your support group? What should you look for, and what should you avoid? Support networks can be incredibly valuable tools, but only if you are smart when drafting your team. While you can receive support from a variety of places and people, and it can come in many different forms, there are certain qualities that should be shared by the people you rely on. For one, you should enjoy the company of whoever you choose. This seems like a no brainer, but many people allow themselves to tolerate spending time with those they dislike because they believe it will provide them with more authentic feedback. In reality, you are just opening yourself up for unhelpful criticism and advice you will be resistant to hearing regardless of its quality or validity. It is much easier to take advice from someone you like than someone you don't, and you can disregard good advice if you simply don't agree with the person giving it. Even if someone is at the top of their field in the area of your goal, they should not be part of your support network unless you truly value their opinions. Filling your group with people you lack a meaningful connection with is more likely to result in bickering and endless disagreements than it is to produce any meaningful aid for your goals.

Once you have narrowed down your pool to people you respect and want to spend time with, consider who best fits the roles you need filled. The people in your support network should be honest, hardworking, and share your values. In short, they should be good people that encourage you to be a better person. Members of your support network should be open and willing to share their information and tips for success. Someone may know everything there is to know about achieving your goal, but if they won't tell you any of it, then they are not helping you learn and grow. Look for those that have done work in your area and whose success you would like to emulate. Finally, include people who inspire you. If you look for people who fit these criteria, your social network will be a close-knit group willing to provide you with the support you need to be at your best.

Great People

Surround yourself with people of good moral character that you honestly enjoy being around. The people in your support network should demonstrate great human qualities and encourage you to demonstrate the same qualities. Those who achieve great success are commendable, but those who do so by bringing others up with them rather than putting them down or stepping on others to achieve their goals are the most admirable and great additions to your team. You can be confident that these types of people are always willing to help you and others out and that they will not purposefully keep you from meeting your goals, whether by putting you down or by withholding information because they are insecure in their success. Great people will be happy to help when they are needed and tend to improve your mindset because of their kind outlooks.

Seek out people who display exceptional qualities and who lift up those around them merely by being around them. This may include being friendly, honest, sincere, and respectful to everyone they meet. They are also likely to lead by example, remain generous regardless of their current level of financial success, engage in healthy lifestyle behaviors, maintain healthy and positive relationships, and remain optimistic when facing new challenges. These are behaviors and habits that help to elevate them into the top 10 percent of achievers. Their good qualities will inspire you to emulate them, and in doing so, you will bring yourself closer to success while never losing touch with your morals and values.

Open and Sharing

You need people who are going to be honest with you as well as those who are eager to share their own experiences. Honesty is often the best policy, and that is especially true when determining who should be in your support network. If someone in your network is dishonest, they can end up impeding your progress by providing you with false encouragement or unnecessary criticism. They may be overly positive just for the sake of not hurting your feelings, and while this may seem like a considerate act at first, it prevents you from noticing when you are on the wrong path before failure has occurred. If you make a decision that others believe may complicate the process of achieving your goals rather than making things more comfortable, they should be able to tell you rather than blindly accepting it as a good decision. Never be afraid to fail, but it is essential to learn from your mistakes so that you can avoid future failures. Having someone who only ever praises you and does not give you the constructive feedback you need is just as detrimental as someone who constantly brings negativity into your life.

You should also choose people who are very open about their own experiences. Even if someone is at the top of their field, they cannot help you if they do not choose to share their information. Many successful people may be worried about others passing them if they give out their secrets to success, so they purposely obfuscate and avoid giving out the advice that matters. This is not the kind of success you want to achieve, nor is it the kind of person you want to be. Your support network should provide you with clear answers about what worked for them and what to avoid. Choosing people for your support network that are willing to help you on your journey so you can be as successful as possible will encourage you to fill that role for others once you have the same experience under your belt. This will allow you to improve your positive impact on the world.

Additionally, you should avoid anyone unwilling

to discuss their own failures out of a sense of pride. Anyone who has achieved great success likely has experienced great failure and those who claim otherwise negatively impact your ability to accept and learn from failure. If you do not realize how often other successful people have failed, you may be tempted to give up once you experience it rather than pushing forward. Instead, look for those who are ready to guide you by explaining their failures, what they learned from them, and how to avoid them in your endeavors.

When you build your network, consider the importance and value they bring to you and how you can return that value and knowledge of not only their experiences, but yours to others who are also seeking mentors to assist them.

Role Models

Single out people who have achieved the specific goals you want to achieve. If you are trying to start a business, look for those who have started their own businesses. If you are trying to run a marathon, seek out those who have run marathons. You should always be on the lookout for like-minded people who can use their own firsthand experience to inform you of the best habits and actions to incorporate into your daily life. Because we all have different aspirations, no one person will share all of the goals you want to achieve, but many will share one or two of the goals that you are pursuing. Keep these people close and learn from them whenever possible.

One way to find people with similar goals is through the use of mastermind groups. A mastermind group "is where a group of people come together to offer mutual support in a specific area of life or business. The group works on synergy whereby the power of the group is more powerful than the sum of its parts" ("Building a Support Network," n.d., para. 6). Mastermind groups are a bit like study groups or support groups in that each member helps others to succeed while learning valuable information from other members at the same time. Many of the people you encounter in a mastermind group will start out as strangers, but over time, as you face challenges together and collaborate on your goals, you will form lasting bonds with your group members. Mastermind groups are an excellent resource for locating and networking with people who care deeply about the same things you do.

Inspirations

Your support circle should ultimately be made up of people who inspire you. Look for optimistic, ambitious people to add to your network who frequently seek to have a positive impact on the world. By surrounding yourself with these types of people, you encourage yourself to emulate them and reach the same heights. Avoid at all costs those individuals with a "glass half empty" mentality who are always looking for a reason to complain or quit. You should be around people who are looking for every opportunity to succeed, not every excuse for failure. You're aiming for the top 10 percent of achievers, and you do not get far in life by constantly bemoaning your situation. Find people who are in tune with your ideals and align with the positive steps and daily habits you will use to achieve your goals. Fill your ranks with truly inspirational people to benefit your mindset and encourage you to be an inspiration to others.

Avoiding Anchors

The choices you make regarding who you choose to spend your time with can be the difference between anchoring yourself in place or sailing towards success. Avoid supposed friends who seem to put you down or question your abilities at every turn. If someone is discouraging you from pursuing your goals, honestly consider whether spending more time with them is doing more harm than good. People in your life who display little interest in having a positive impact, have few aspirations, make poor decisions for their health, wealth, friendships and wellbeing and show you no support are not the role models you need if you want to truly achieve success. They will essentially become an anchor for your journey, keeping you from making forward progress, and exploring the open ocean waters of the world.

Instead, spend your time with friends, family, and colleagues who are positive, exciting, and have great outlooks on life. These people will inspire you to be better and improve your own outlook. They will be in your corner, supporting you and encouraging you to achieve your goals, rather than holding you back. These people are the sails that allow you to harness the winds of progress and change, taking you out of safe waters and guiding you through the open ocean towards your goals. With their help, you can experience a world of opportunity and excitement.

Jim Rohan, international motivational speaker and author once said that you are the average of the five people you spend the most time with. If you spend time with people with negative outlooks and no desire to achieve their goals, you may become negative in turn. If you spend time with people who lift you up and relentlessly pursue their own goals, you will do the same.

Chapter summary:

- Develop a support network that provides you with resources, moral support, and advice
- Choose your team based on who would be best suited to support your personal brand
- Establish a meaningful personal connection with everyone on your team
- Seek out great people who share your values and will support your vision and goals.
- People in your network should be willing to share information about both their successes and their failures
- Look for people who are high achievers in your field and encourage you to adopt likeminded daily habits.
- Inspirational people will encourage you to be the best version of yourself
- Avoid anchors or those who have negative outlooks and keep you from reaching your goals and success

Overview:

Remember the Rules

You have all the resources you need to succeed. Now, you must simply put them into action, keeping in mind everything you have learned so far. Your future success is dependent on your ability to adhere to these rules and make the best use of everything you have learned. Remember that your goals, wishes, and dreams are all possible so long as you remain committed, follow the steps outlined in this book, and maintain a success mindset. Come back to this section to review the rules for success whenever you need guidance on your next step in your journey to success.

The Rules of Success

1. Have complete clarity on what you want

Fully understand what you want and why you want it. Being unclear on your goals is the best way to lose sight of them as soon as difficulties arise. Take time to consider what your ideal life would look like and what goals you would need to accomplish to achieve it. If you know what you are after and how each goal will benefit your life, you are less likely to give up and more likely to successfully push past adversity.

2. Don't overcomplicate your goals

Keep your goals simple and relevant to your desires. Start with small, short-term goals and use them to build up to bigger goals over time. Less complicated goals will help you realize how much progress you are making with every step. You don't need to have goals that impact the rest of the world; just choose goals that matter to you, and your positive impact on those around you will follow.

3. Write your goals down and take immediate action

You cannot accomplish anything if you never start moving. Write your goals down to give you a direction and purpose, and then take actions that bring you closer to those goals. Keep moving and always keep your desired end result in mind.

4. Ensure you have a strong reason attached to each goal

Know the reason why you want to accomplish each of your goals. Think about the ways it will bring you closer to your dream life, or how it will pave the way for bigger successes. Have an idea of what kind of person you want to be and how your goals can help you be that person. If you know why you are working, you will never feel like your efforts have been wasted.

5. Establish your plan to achieve your goals

Once you know where you are going, come up with the path to get there. Work backward from your goals to devise the steps you will need to take. Your plan will take these steps and turn them into productive daily habits that bring you closer to your goals each day. With a clear and detailed roadmap to guide you, you are sure to achieve success.

6. Develop a timeline for each goal

Figure out how long each goal is going to take you to complete. Is it a big goal that may require a year or more to complete? Is it a five-year stretch goal that will set the tone for the smaller, more manageable goals it is comprised of? For smaller goals, can you get them done in a week, a month, or half a year? Decide what is realistic for you while still encouraging you to get moving and set that date as the deadline. Adhering to the deadlines you have imposed on yourself will ensure you are keeping a good schedule and practicing good time management.

7. Implement daily visualization to embed your goals in your subconscious

Take time each day to picture what a successful future looks like and how living that life would make you feel. Remind yourself of what you are working for and what you are willing to do to achieve it. Visualization is one of the most powerful tools you have at your disposal.

8. Implement supportive daily habits and structures

Take steps each day to keep yourself on the right track. Develop a to-do list of daily habits that you must complete by the end of the day. Commit yourself to these habits, and in time they will become second nature. Good daily habits are the basic structure of a productive day, week, month, and year.

9. Surround yourself with positive and supportive people

Make sure those around you are as committed to your success as you are. Limit spending time with people who doubt you or want to keep you right where you are, and start spending it with people who will encourage you to reach for your dreams. The people you surround yourself with have a massive impact on what type of person you want to be, so make sure you are seeking good influences as often as possible.

10. Make a commitment for daily action

Work hard every single day in pursuit of your goals. This does not infer that you '*physically*' work every day, rather, work hard on your growth through knowledge acquisition and your supportive daily habits. We all need time for vacations with our friends, loved ones or to develop fresh and innovative ideas. There is no excuse worth breaking your forward momentum. If you take action every day and you are wholeheartedly committed to achieving success, your hopes and dreams are within your grasp.

Conclusion

The **7-step plan** outlined above supplies you with everything you need to begin setting goals, making strides towards achieving them, establish supportive daily habits, all combining to provide the momentum you need. You can accomplish the things you have always wanted in life so long as you know what your goals are and why you want to achieve them. The path ahead of you now may be difficult, and it may require more work than you have ever put into something before. It will likely test the limits of your commitment and your resolve as you push yourself to heights you never imagined you could achieve. You will have moments of doubt, uncertainty, and setbacks on your path to success. But when you finally achieve what you desire most, all the work you have put in to get where you need to be will have been worth it. Establishing healthy methods and structures in your life and persevering in the face of adversity will turn you into someone who sees what they want and has the ability and willpower to reach out and take it.

Throughout this book, you have learned the tools you will need to go out and achieve real success. You now know the importance of believing in yourself and your abilities, as well as developing a forward-thinking mindset that opens you up to so many possibilities. You have freed yourself from the shackles of your limiting beliefs. DR. ACTION™ has helped you to utilize action in the service of self-improvement and time management. You have established habits, created daily structure, and developed a firm understanding of your motivations that all future actions will build upon. You understand the value of having a strong foundation in this regard. You know the difference between supportive habits and those that work against your ability to succeed. Not only do you have the resolve not to give up when you encounter tough times, but you also know not to fear failure and instead embrace it and use it as a learning experience. Your forward momentum will carry you through to success no matter how many times you stumble on the way there. The Goal Loop strategy has taught you how to turn your celebration into productivity and motivation to tackle bigger and better objectives.

You now understand how to make decisions with your future in mind, including who you choose to surround yourself with. Filling your life with productive and like-minded individuals who you respect and appreciate will encourage you to succeed and leave a positive impact on those around you. Finally, you know the rules to success and how to implement them in optimal ways to guarantee you achieve your goals.

Start Now

With all this information, you are now capable of overcoming any obstacles in your way. Nothing will keep you down for long. If you truly desire to change your life through the achievement of meaningful goals, you will take the first step today to put these practices into action. Make the most of the time available to you and start drafting your goals, formulating daily habits, and visualizing your achievements.

You are responsible for making decisions that will allow you to achieve your goals. It is up to you to keep your life on the right track, which means you must keep your end goal in mind to arrive at the right place. A clear picture of your future will empower you to fully understand the consequences of each decision, right or wrong, and guide you towards making the right decisions. Whether you recognize it in the moment or years later, every decision you have made in life up to this point has had a direct impact on the life you now live. Every success and every failure, every path of study and every late assignment, every utilized opportunity and every missed one has contributed to the result of your life. You have the power to improve your situation, whether you set your sights on relationships with friends and family, milestones like the purchase of your first car, traveling, religious commitments, your health and fitness, continued education, decreasing alcohol consumption, your employment, or any other area of your life.

I see some people spend their whole lives waiting for the right moment to pursue their goals. They spend so long waiting that they let opportunities pass them by entirely unnoticed, and by the end of their years they look back and wish they had paid more attention to the chances the universe presented to them. Stop waiting, and don't let another excuse get in the way of your goals whether they be to improve your health, start a new business venture, develop a skill, learn new information, or improve your relationships for a more fulfilling life. The time to take actions is today. Your time is right now!

There is one key factor though that I want you to keep in the forefront of your mind as you proceed with goal setting. If there is a single element I want you to take from Magnetic Goals, it should be that your choices and actions will determine your success. Every opportunity you choose to act on or ignore, every habit you keep practicing or fail to do, every misstep and rebound is a result of your own choices. You should hold yourself accountable for your success and not wait around for it to happen. This is why it is so important to take action now. While you may have many friends and supportive colleagues cheering you on and rooting for your success, only you can ensure you reach the finish line. You owe it to your support network and to yourself to make choices that keep you pushing towards achieving your goals.

"The decisions you make and the actions you take will define your success."

As you get the ball rolling and begin to succeed, future goals will become even easier to achieve. Success provides a huge compounding energy for more success, and the tools and skills you learn whilst accomplishing your first smaller goals will leave you better equipped to tackle the challenges of your long-term goals. The purpose of Magnetic Goals is to build knowledge, expertise and momentum so you can continue to improve and succeed. The more goals you achieve, the more momentum you will build and the more magnetic your goals will be. If you remain committed to your goals, follow the steps outlined in this book, and never lose your hunger for improving yourself, you will become a true *success magnet*!

Resources

Beck, M. (2011, September). *Martha Beck's 6-Step Guide to Taming Your Fears.*

Retrieved December 30, 2019, from http://www.oprah.com/spirit/overcoming-fear-how-to-conquer-your-fears_4

Building a Support Network. (n.d.). Retrieved December 30, 2019, from https://www.coachingpositiveperformance.com/building-a-support-network/

Burnford, J. (2019, January 30). *Limiting Beliefs: What Are They And How Can You Overcome Them?* Retrieved December 30, 2019, from https://www.forbes.com/

sites/joyburnford/2019/01/30/limiting-beliefs-what-are-they-and-how-can-you-overcome-them/#626ef8836303

Clear, J. (n.d.-a). *How To Start New Habits That Actually Stick.* Retrieved December 30, 2019, from https://jamesclear.com/three-steps-habit-change

Clear, J. (n.d.-b). *The Habits Guide: How to Build Good Habits and Break Bad Ones.* Retrieved December 30, 2019, from https://jamesclear.com/habits

Create a Timeline for your Goal. (2015). Retrieved December 30, 2019, from http://www.skillstoolbox.com/personal-skills/goal-setting/goal-setting-process/create-a-timeline-for-your-goal/

Department of Health & Human Services. (n.d.). *Physical activity - it's important.* Retrieved December 30, 2019,

from
https://www.betterhealth.vic.gov.au/health/healthyliving
/physical-activity-its-important

Dewe, C. (2019). *How To Improve Your Life By Discovering Your Why.* Retrieved December 30, 2019, from
https://www.lifehack.org/articles/productivity/how-improve-your-life-discovering-your-why.html

Dulin, D. (2015). *The Importance of Visualizing your Goals.* Retrieved December 30, 2019, from
https://www.unfinishedsuccess.com/the-importance-of-visualizing-your-goals/

Dweck, C. (2016, January 13). *What Having a "Growth Mindset" Actually Means.* Retrieved December 30, 2019, from https://hbr.org/2016/01/what-having-a-growth-mindset-actually-means

Efron, L. (2019, March 27). *Kindness: Does Being Kind to Others Help you Live Longer?* Retrieved December 30, 2019, from
https://www.developgoodhabits.com/kindness-live-longer/

Erwin, M. (2015, September 8). *When You Fall, Fall Forward: Why Failure is Essential To Success.* Retrieved December 30, 2019, from
https://www.linkedin.com/pulse/when-you-fall-forward-why-failure-essential-success-mark-erwin

Eschenroeder, K. (2014). *The Overthinker's Guide for Taking Action: A Complete Guide.* Retrieved December 30, 2019, from https://startupbros.com/

overthinkers-guide-taking-action-complete-guide/Fahkry,

T. (2017, September 25). *These 6 Powerful Ways Will Help You Overcome*

Obstacles And Reclaim Your Power. Retrieved December 30, 2019, from https://medium.com/the-mission/these-6-powerful-ways-will-help-you-overcome-obstacles-and-reclaim-your-power-b1fabdb8e074

Happy Living. (n.d.). *The Importance of Gratitude*. Retrieved December 30, 2019, from https://happysnackcompany.com.au/importance-of-gratitude/

Herzing Staff. (n.d.). *Why Your Support System Is Important for Your Success*. Retrieved December 30, 2019, from https://www.herzing.edu/blog/why-your-support-system-important-your-success

Janeksela, J. (2018, January 3). *Why You Should Make Visualization a Daily Practice*. Retrieved December 30, 2019, from https://www.success.com/why-you-should-make-visualization-a-daily-practice/

Johnson, S. (2014). *How Can I Make a Positive Impact in Others' Lives?* Retrieved December 30, 2019, from https://www.insightforliving.ca/read/articles/q-how-can-i-make-positive-impact-others-lives

Lauby, S. (2016, February 2). *How to Set a Relevant Goal*. Retrieved December 30, 2019, from https://www.people-doc.com/blog/how-to-set-a-relevant-goal

Lickus, J. (2014, July 28). *10 Simple Ways To Make The Most Of Your Time*. Retrieved December 30, 2019, from https://www.huffpost.com/entry/time-management-tips-_b_5365403

Mayo Clinic Staff. (2019, May 11). *Exercise: 7 benefits of regular physical activity*. Retrieved December 30, 2019, from https://www.mayoclinic.org/healthy-lifestyle/fitness/in-depth/exercise/art-20048389

Menon, S. (2019, November 25). *Rich Pickings: How to invest in yourself and save money in the long run*. Retrieved December 30, 2019, from https://gulfnews.com/how-to/your-money/rich-pickings-how-to-invest-in-yourself-and-save-money-in-the-long-run-1.1574678488159

Mind Tools content team. (2016). *Overcoming Fear of Failure: Facing Your Fear of Moving Forward*. Retrieved December 30, 2019, from https://www.mindtools.com/pages/article/fear-of-failure.htm

Sinek, S. (n.d.). *The Science of Why*. Retrieved December 30, 2019, from https://simonsinek.com/find-your-why/

Spring, S. (2018, March 3). *How To Motivate Yourself To Take Action Today*. Retrieved December 30, 2019, from https://medium.com/live-your-life-on-purpose/how-to-motivate-yourself-to-take-action-this-week-9df6dd89e3e9

SUCCESS. (2016, August 25). *Why Failure Is Good for Success*. Retrieved December 30, 2019, from https://www.success.com/why-failure-is-good-for-success/

The Oracles. (2018, December 7). *"Most people probably would have stopped" — 8 tips on overcoming even the most crippling setbacks*. Retrieved December 30, 2019,

from https://www.cnbc.com/2018/12/07/8-tips-on-overcoming-even-the-most-crippling-setbacks.html

Tracy, B. (2008). *The Law of Clarity*. Retrieved December 30, 2019, from https://www.briantracy.com/blog/leadership-success/the-law-of-clarity/

Tracy, B. (2014). *My Best Tips on How to Stop Procrastinating*. Retrieved December 30, 2019, from https://www.briantracy.com/blog/time-management/how-to-

stop-procrastinating-time-management-organizational-skills/Tracy, B. (2017). *Million Dollar Habits: Proven Power Practices to Double and Triple*

Your Income. Irvine, California: Entrepreneur Press.

Vocabulary.com. (n.d.-a). *Commitment - Dictionary Definition*. Retrieved December 30, 2019, from https://www.vocabulary.com/dictionary/commitment

Vocabulary.com. (n.d.-b). *Enthusiasm - Dictionary Definition*. Retrieved December 30, 2019, from https://www.vocabulary.com/dictionary/enthusiasm?family=Enthusiasm

Winfield, C. (2018, September 7). *The Ultimate Guide to Becoming Your Best Self: Build your Daily Routine by Optimizing Your Mind, Body and Spirit*. Retrieved December 30, 2019, from https://open.buffer.com/daily-success-routine/

The Habit Switch

How Little Changes Can Produce Massive Results for Your Health, Diet and Energy Levels by Introducing Incremental Mini Habits

ROMNEY NELSON

INTRODUCTION

How amazing would it be if it was as simple as flicking a switch to suddenly change your health and fitness habits for good! What if this was possible? What if it required just small daily changes to your current lifestyle, rather than radical changes that are unlikely to have a long term and positive impact?

What I'm about to show you will prove that with just small and incremental daily changes and the right systems, *you can* transform your health and fitness habits for good, but on one condition.... you must switch your mindset from short term to long term thinking.

Welcome to The Habit Switch. My name is Romney Nelson, and I want to provide you with all the knowledge to help make a transformation with how you view your fitness and health.

To provide you with some details of my background, I have a significant wealth of experience in health, fitness and wellbeing. I have a Bachelor of Physical Education & Health, and I have been Head of Faculty for some of the leading

Independent Schools in Australia and the UK. I am a qualified Personal Trainer and coach; I have represented Australia at the World Championships in Hong Kong for Dragon Boat Racing and have participated in the National Championships for Surf Life Saving.

I have complimented my sporting achievements with an extensive employment career. I have served on several Executive Teams and National positions of responsibility. I have worked for the Australian Football League (AFL) and currently have a seat on the Advisory Board of Australia's largest mobile dental provider with over 40,000 patients per year. My personal experience in the fields of health, exercise physiology and sports training has provided me with the opportunity to share all that I have learned to help you regain control over your eating habits and physical fitness.

I wrote The Habit Switch with a key focus to guide you through the methods to build the right systems, structures and mindset to help you determine what advice is real and what advice is pure marketing in the billion-dollar fitness and dieting industry. Further to this, *The Habit Switch* will provide you with all the information that will enable you to significantly improve your diet, health and fitness in a simplified and easy to implement system.

We gravitate towards books that will help us.

There's a reason why you are reading this book and it's because we all want to improve our diet and fitness to keep ourselves healthy, but it seems like every day there is a new article with an entirely different way to go about it. It is easy to have the best intentions when starting a new diet routine but still find yourself falling victim to confusing marketing practices that are only trying to achieve short-term success without caring if their methods are effective for the long term.

Diet and exercise plans that help you lose a few pounds very quickly are effective in the short term, but they often lose steam the longer you follow them. Some diets are simply too restrictive to follow for more than a few weeks, leaving you lethargic, hungry and craving something more substantial, ultimately leading you towards ending the diet. Other diet plans ask for a significant commitment of time and combining this with very busy lives; they tend to fall by the wayside. Dropping an exercise plan or not getting the right results on a diet can make you feel unnecessarily guilty, but the truth is, the lack of success on these plans is due to the focus on the short term rather than more powerful and lasting long-term results.

Additionally, due to the abundance of different diet plans, health and fitness advice from various sources can often vary greatly. The information these sources suggest can even contradict other fitness books and articles, leaving you uncertain about what will really work to improve your health. One study will claim that frequent alcohol consumption leads to health problems, while another will tell you to have a glass of red wine every day. Some sources tell you to eat more fat, while others suggest you to stop eating fat altogether. The same is true for whether or not you should be eating red meat and incorporating designated 'superfoods' into your diet. Even health suggestions that are not contradictory can become overwhelming due to the sheer number of factors you must keep track of. Altering your diet, counting your steps, reducing your calories, keeping track of macros, drinking more water, and dozens of other measures ask for an unrealistically significant contribution of your time and energy, which can be especially frustrating when you see minimal results even after all of that work. With all of this in mind, it is no surprise that it is hard to narrow down precisely what you should and shouldn't be doing to get and stay healthy. But what is the solution to cutting through all the confusion and figuring out what works?

Improving your health needs to become natural, and you need to feel comfortable with the process. Adopting a diet and exercise regimen that benefits your body and mind is instead a gradual process of improving your daily habits and allowing them to build incrementally to create real change.

Healthy Habits

Habits are the little actions we take every day, even without thinking about them, that make up our daily routines. Small habits can have a surprisingly large impact on your life. Their strength lies in the fact that they promote constant action in your subconscious, letting you break down a difficult task into more manageable segments and complete it over a length of time. For example, say you want to write a novel. Trying to write thousands of words each day would certainly be a formidable task. However, if you simply committed yourself to write a mere 200 words a day, a habit which fits more easily into your schedule, you would make progress on your book every day. The act of writing would become habitual over time, and with steady progress, you would finish your book much sooner than you once thought possible. Habits can be applied to every part of your life, including health and fitness, and making good use of them can yield amazing results.

Adopting healthy habits means leaving behind unhealthy ones. These bad habits likely started small with minimal impact on your physical fitness, but over time they grew to become serious problems. One white chocolate and blueberry muffin on occasions is not a big deal, but when that muffin turns into one every day, it becomes a bad habit that can prevent you from getting healthier. Weight gain can be a product of just a small amount of excess calories over a long period of time. However, just as small negative habits can cause health problems, small diet changes and increases in physical activity can keep you from gaining weight and counteract the effects of unhealthy behaviors. In either case, your health is not a product of single decisions but rather the sum of all of your habits over time. The solution that is most effective for weight loss then, is starting small and reversing the negative habits you have picked up over the years.

Small, constructive habits have more long-term benefits than attempting to change everything about your lifestyle all at once. Trying to make too great of a change in a short period is likely to lead to exhaustion and a loss of willpower, leaving you right back where you started. Instead, try introducing habits that are easy to complete and don't take up too much of your time. These easily manageable tasks let you make progress on your goals while also training your brain to practice healthy habits each day. Once you are comfortable with the initial habits, you can slowly build upon them. You will find the success you are looking for without the concern of not being able to keep up because you overloaded yourself too early. Once you adopt good habits, improving your health becomes as easy as flipping 'The Habit Switch'.

Flipping the switch

This book will teach you how to flip the switch and turn on positive healthy habits. The first step of your new health solution is a four-part process called STOP>REVIEW>PIVOT and POWER. This system allows you to stop and evaluate your current habits, review the progress or lack of improvement of your current situation, pivot your habits towards those that will help you achieve your goals, and then power through to success. The right mindset is also critical to ensuring the decisions you make today will positively impact your health tomorrow.

The Habit Switch will provide you with:

- An understanding of the powerful Stop, Review, Pivot, and Power system
- Tips for establishing a mindset of positivity and focus
- Specific, actionable steps and mini habits you can

implement that, when compounded over time, lead to exponential benefits for your diet, fitness, and energy levels.

- The reason why "no pain, no gain" is wrong and how you can achieve incredible long-term gains by flipping the switch on this mentality.
- An appreciation that the role of exercise and supportive eating habits can have for a long term and sustainable approach.

You can achieve change without any of the difficulties associated with extreme dieting, excessive exercise and adjusting your lifestyle too quickly. All it takes is a series of small steps and the dedication to make a change in your life.

With *The Habit Switch,* you can completely revolutionize your mindset through the development and implementation of mini habits. You will learn how so many people have been manipulated by marketing in the fitness industry. You will also learn why it's time to introduce a sensible and bulletproof strategy for mastering your health habits, starting with incremental changes and leading to huge changes in your life. Implementing the mini habits introduced to you in this book will unlock lifelong positive changes.

You can experience higher levels of energy, have greater productivity, maintain a healthy body weight, and become knowledgeable about behaviors and foods that are healthy for your mind as well as your body. The daily exercise and fitness habits you develop will be long-term and sustainable, not just shortcuts and quick fix changes that are likely to fall apart under pressure. The changes you will be encouraged to make through daily habits will really stick.

You have spent enough time searching through endless diet and exercise plans that never get you the results you deserve. *The Habit Switch* is the resource you have been waiting for. It will provide you with a sustainable approach that doesn't stop at short-term results but rather, will yield long-term success. It is time to start making changes and adopting habits that will help you become the best version of yourself, and it all starts with you. The decisions you make and the actions you take will lead you down the path to living a happier, healthier and more fulfilling life.

I think it is time that you are provided with a no-nonsense and honest guide that isn't full of shortcuts promising changes in 7 days, rather, a book that provides actionable steps that can be implemented over time that will build the foundation for long term success. You must be open to change, and it begins with a commitment to taking small steps now that will result in giant leaps later on.

Chapter 1

My Habits

The Mindset and Systems for a Healthy Body

Changing your daily habits is a powerful tool, but it can be difficult to know where to start. When figuring out which habits you should prioritize to improve your health, it is helpful to have an example of a good set of habits. I want to provide you with my personal list of habits that I do every day to ensure I am making progress towards my goals. I believe that supplying you with this information will give you a template to base your

200

habits off and help you define what you want to achieve and the way you want to achieve it. Everyone's individual habits are going to be different; your daily habits should be reflective of what you value, what you want to improve, and the time you can commit to each goal. By sharing my habits, I hope to guide you through the process I used to select my own habits and show how they each support my endeavors.

My personal mantra is "What can I do today that will further my personal growth and move me closer to reaching my full potential tomorrow?" Every day should bring you closer to reaching your potential. As you will find out as you read this book, I don't advocate for perfectionism, but rather personal fulfilment. You should strive to become the best possible version of yourself, not someone else. This means following your own dreams, not the goals someone else has set for you. As a result, I develop my habits based on my personal goals because they are made up of the things that I want for myself and my family. This includes my physical health as well as my mental well-being. Our bodies are the vehicles we need to achieve all of our goals, so we owe it to ourselves to look after the gift and opportunity we have been given.

How I Established My Habit Schedule

My habit schedule is influenced by who I am as a person. People who know me well appreciate that I am well-structured, organized and very focused. I also consider myself to be committed to the goals I set for myself. As a result, I schedule my habits with the aim to do them at the same time every day. Having a schedule to fall back on reinforces positive behaviors and helps me keep track of my progress. Because of this, I have scheduled my habits in a way that allows me to maximize their benefits and give them an appropriate amount of time. I make sure to avoid rushing a new or developing habit so that it "takes root" firmly and develops correctly. I try to take each action seriously and give them time to develop incrementally so that I don't overwhelm myself.

My diet is one area that I pay careful attention to. A healthy, nutritious diet provides me with the energy I need to accomplish all of my other goals, so I need to ensure I am keeping myself in the best possible shape. I would consider my diet to be well balanced, mainly as a result of my upbringing, my background in sports, and my qualifications in physical education and health. I always want to embody what I suggest for others. If I encourage others to eat certain foods and maintain a balanced diet or to exercise a certain way, it's because I do it myself. Of course, I also think it is important to highlight that I do still drift on occasions from a diet of nutritious foods. I still have the occasional pizza, a beer with family and friends, a good coffee, and even a great muffin. These little treats can be nice to enjoy now and then. However, I try to keep them to a minimum in my diet. My personal eating habits restrict less healthy foods to around five percent of my overall diet. This leaves plenty of room for more nutritious options most days, which bring me closer to my goals of living a long and healthy life. I fill the rest of my diet with healthy foods that provide my body with the fuel I need to take me to my 100th birthday.

Exercise is another important part of my routine. It is a habit that I picked up when I was younger while training for competitive sports, which also left me with a few niggling injuries. I am lucky that only one, a bulging disk in my neck from a gymnastics injury, impacts my mobility on occasions so that I can do most physical exercises. However, I recognize that this is not true for everyone and that as we age, exercise becomes about finding sustainable activities we can integrate into our lives without increasing the chance of injury. Many friends of mine who have sustained injuries during competitive sports and long-distance running do have limitations with their mobility. When finding the right exercise for you, it is critical to take into account your limitations and choose something you can do on a regular basis.

Ultimately, my habits are structured to provide long-term support and assistance on my journey to reach my goals, which is the same idea you should take into account when deciding on your own habits. I will expand on the methods I use to narrow down the habits that best suit my lifestyle throughout the book, as well as how I began implementing these habits and building them incrementally so they can build up to compounding effects over time. However, I want to provide a word of warning first. The habits that work well for me may not be suitable for you. I am using my personal schedule in the book primarily to illustrate the power of habits and what they allow you to do, not to suggest you copy my habits directly. They are suited to my own long-term goals, but they may not be reflective of yours. Spend some time thinking about what you want to achieve and how you would be able to go about achieving it as you create your own list of daily supportive habits.

My Morning Routine

Detailing every single habit I do each day would take a great deal of time, so I have limited my scope to just my morning routine, which I hope serves as an introduction and a template for your own. Use it to get an idea of my structure and how I have been able to incorporate ten healthy and supportive habits over 2 hours.

- **4:25 AM** - Wake up
- **4:30 AM** - Power walk with my dog and listen to an educational podcast
- **5:05 AM** - Drink 500 mL water and take one

magnesium supplement

- **5:07 AM** - Breakfast of porridge with fresh fruit and one scoop of natural yoghurt
- **5:16 AM** - 120 push-ups (4 sets of 30)
- **5:20 AM** - 200 sit-ups (4 sets of 50)
- **5:30 AM** - Personal daily goal affirmations (recorded and played back)
- **5:35 AM** - Meditation and visualization for 15 minutes
- **5:50 AM** - The Daily Goal Tracker: record what I'm grateful for, my current thoughts, and three key actions
- **6:00 AM** – Shower
- **6:15 AM** - Reading for 20 minutes
- **6:35 AM** - Begin the day

These habits are short activities that take up a small portion of my day. They are not too difficult for me to complete, which means I have no trouble repeating them each morning. Over the course of one month, assuming I do these habits six days a week and use Sunday as my rest and recovery day, they build up to a powerful transformation. Here is the massive compounding impact I receive by the end of the month:

- Walking/exercise = **12 hrs.**
- Podcasts (inspirational interviews) = **12 hrs.**
- Push-ups = **2,880** push-ups for upper body strength and tone
- Sit-ups = **4,800** sit-ups for core strength and avoiding lower back pain
- Planting my goals subconsciously via daily affirmations = **2 hrs.**
- Meditation/visualization = **8 hrs.**
- Prioritization of daily activities to move closer to my goals = **72** key actions
- Journaling six things I am grateful for daily = **24** days of journaling
- Reading = **8 hrs.**

You can now see just how much of an impact mini habits can have on your life. If I simply decided to do 4,800 sit-ups in a month without any other planning, I would likely end up slacking some days and failing to reach my goal. By breaking the process up into more bite-sized, easily achievable sections each day, I have no trouble reaching my goal. I hope that you can use this process of establishing mini habits to achieve the same levels of tremendous change and amazing results for your health, diet, and energy levels.

Chapter 2

Compound Growth
+
Mini Habits = Big Impact

Part one of *The Habit Switch* is all about transformation. How is transformation possible, what sort of mindset do you need to adopt to encourage change, and how will you devise your plan to improve your life? Understanding the habit switch process will help you answer all of these questions.

This section will help you begin to identify the areas you want to improve in that matter to you personally. You should always work towards goals that you care about rather than what is expected of you; doing so will provide the necessary motivation to keep up with your new schedule. The section will also discuss the benefits you can see if you stick to mini habits over a long period of time, which can build to amazing results that would have felt near-impossible to tackle all at once. With the power of small changes, you can completely turn your health and fitness around.

Part of making changes is developing a plan that will take you from your first steps all the way to your goals. By identifying where you want to end up, you can establish the steps you will take to keep you on the right track, aligned with your values, and turning negative habits into positive ones. Great goal setting, aided by my method of DR. ACTION™, will help you organize your habits in a way that encourages you to always keep moving forward and keeps you from faltering on your path to success. But before you can do that, you must understand what it takes to make a transformative change.

What Does It Take to Transform?

Changing your mindset is the key to changing your life. The wrong mindset can keep you stuck in the same situation for months or even years, unable to make changes that stick despite your best intentions. The right mindset, on the other hand, can make you see every opportunity the universe throws your way in a new light. It will help you develop confidence and maintain your commitment to reaching success. Mindset then is imperative to a real transformation.

There has been a great deal of research into the different kinds of mindset, and one school of thought is that of the static mindset and the development mindset. Static mindset suggests that you are predisposed towards certain qualities, through your nature or some other innate skill, and the things you can excel in are for the most part set in stone. A development mindset, on the other hand, means you believe you can grow and expand your skills with effort and experience. While the static mindset can allow you to improve in certain areas, it suggests that you are not capable of improving in all areas, or those that you do not initially excel at. This means it can be harder to change bad habits and try new things, as you believe you simply cannot get any better if you don't show an immediate aptitude for something. A static mindset attempts to dissuade you from change.

A development mindset promotes attempting new things, possibly failing but always showing improvement with each step of your journey. In short, it encourages moving forward and branching out. This is what makes a development mindset so powerful. When you believe you are capable of getting better at a task or activity, you will give yourself more time to keep pushing at something that is difficult for you rather than giving up when your first attempts do not lead to success. You can allow yourself to find the fitness habits that work for you and avoid falling into the trap of thinking that if you do not see instant results, you will never see them.

If you currently operate under a static mindset, start shifting your thoughts over to a development mindset instead. You can accomplish this through a few different ways, the first of which involves accepting the possibility of failure. Remember that no failure needs to be permanent and that faltering can give us the experience and tools we need to succeed. Additionally, you can start to prioritize the journey of growth over the destination. While you always want to be moving towards your goals, there is a lot to enjoy in the process of improving as well, so don't forget to celebrate the little milestones along the way. It is also essential to keep the reasons why you are seeking change in the forefront of your mind. Research suggests that people with development mindsets have a greater sense of purpose, which allows them to maintain focus on the big picture (Briggs, 2015, para. 18). Your sense of purpose, or the reason why you are committed to your goals, will ensure you stick to your habits and successfully transform yourself.

What is transformation?

What does it mean to transform your life, not just make minor tweaks and alterations? What separates a temporary, unsustainable burst of movement from something more permanent? To know the difference, you need to have a good idea of what transformation is and what it is not.

Cambridge Dictionary's definition of the word transformational is "able to produce a big change or improvement in a situation" (Cambridge Dictionary, n.d., para. 2). Let's break this definition down into its parts to get a better understanding.

Firstly, something that is transformational is "able," not guaranteed, to produce a change. It may be very likely that a given action, like eating less junk food or doing a few extra sit-ups, will contribute to better health. However, it is not a guarantee if the rest of your habits do not support the change. This is why it is so vital to ensure all of your daily habits are supportive and that you stick to your supportive habits as often as you can.

Transformational actions are likely to lead to a "big change or improvement," not a minimal one. Losing two or three pounds is not much of a transformation, but committing yourself to improve your health is a full-body change that qualifies as a large-scale improvement. To make a transformation, you need to be ready to make lasting changes in the areas that matter.

Finally, transformations involve changes to your

"situation." To expand on this, I'm referring to where you are at currently regarding your mental attitude and physical wellbeing. A real transformation incites change in every aspect of your life. The *STOP>REVIEW>PIVOT* and *POWER* system discussed in later chapters will show you how to assess your current situation and set you off in the direction of improving all areas of importance to you. Remember that your goal is for these changes in your situation to be permanent. To make a lasting change, it is not enough to spend just one week on a crash diet and expect the change to stick. You need to make a long-term commitment to establishing and cultivating new habits.

Making a Long-Term Commitment

Making a lasting healthy change takes time. It is all too tempting to believe that once you start adopting a healthy diet and exercising, that everything will just fall into place. It takes a long-term commitment to change, and a never quit attitude that will provide the results that you desire. If you want to improve, you must accept that a long-lasting change in your health is a product of slow changes over time rather than drastic, unsustainable changes.

Expecting results to occur too quickly can be harmful to your long-term success. It can even point to a subconscious desire to sabotage yourself and give yourself an excuse to give up on extremely strict, difficult diets. Looking for instant change "is a mechanism to make it easy for you to give up. If you know that you have to do something, which is not possible, then you know that it is doomed to fail" (Heijligers, n.d., para. 9) and you can simply quit. You give yourself the excuse to give up because you have created an impossible expectation for yourself. This can mean that no change ever occurs. If you give yourself time to set up a good foundation instead of constantly looking for results, you will be more likely to stick with your fitness plan for as long as it takes those results to appear.

You may also be operating under the belief that if you do not see the change right away, nothing is working. Many diets boast that you can lose five pounds (2kgs) in the first week, or twenty pounds (9 kgs) in twenty days, therefore you go into all diet plans expecting to see immediate results. If you don't see what you expect, this may cause you to drop the diet altogether. In reality, a large portion of lasting change is setting up the groundwork for future benefits. While you may not see immediate results, that does not mean nothing is happening; you are giving yourself the tools to succeed in the future.

Investing in Your Future

The single best investment you can make is in yourself. You need a healthy mind and body that will allow you to achieve everything you desire. Set goals, keep yourself healthy, expand your knowledge, and ultimately be aware of your value. Knowing your knowledge and actions matter is an investment in your morale (Tull, 2017, para. 9). Remaining self-confident and positive will help you keep going when it would be much easier to give up.

Consider what matters most to you, and what are the specific outcomes you are hoping to achieve? Forget what other people want you to do and the expectations they place on you and just consider your desires. In particular, think about the long-term goals that each step of the dieting and exercise process will help you to achieve and select steps that fit your end goals.

The idea of deriving habits from self-defined goals is well-researched and supported in many areas of healthcare. In 2012, Gardner, Lally & Wardle found that if doctors helped patients set their own health goals, it actually supported patients' sense of autonomy and sustained their interest.

Steve Jobs, the co-founder of Apple, summarized it well when he said; *"Your time is limited, so don't waste it living someone else's life. Don't be trapped by dogma – which is living with the results of other people's thinking. Don't let the noise of other's opinions drown out your inner voice. And most important, have the courage to follow your heart and intuition. They somehow already know what you truly want to become. Everything else is secondary."*

Healthy Habit Change
Why Small Is Actually BIG!

Big changes can come from relatively small actions. It would be impossible to completely uproot every behavior pattern you have subconsciously followed for years in a single day. Think of your journey as laying a garden path made of pavers. You will need to lay one paver at a time as this will allow the next paver to fit to create your pattern. You will start slow, ensuring you have a solid foundation to build from. As you lay more pavers, it becomes easier, your momentum builds, and your skills grow. So, start with the first paver - that is, begin laying the foundation for your health overhaul with small habits that will eventually lead to a considerable change in behavior.

Habits are so small that they often go unnoticed unless you are consciously looking for them. You may perform a bad habit, like grabbing a takeaway iced coffee with lunch every day without thinking twice about it. The problem comes when these small actions build-up, and without realizing it, you have had an iced coffee every day for months or years at a time. The solution involves exchanging these bad habits for good ones and conditioning yourself to develop a different response to the same stimulus.

Your surroundings and environment also have a

considerable influence on your actions. Being in a particular location, seeing the clock hit a specific time of day, and taking a certain action can all be triggers for different habits. Every time you encounter stimulus A, you perform action B. This behavior, carried out over a period of time, is how a habit is formed. Even the act of brushing your teeth after the stimulus of waking up in the morning is a habit that has been cultivated over years of practice. When you get into the habit of making the right choice after encountering a given stimulus, you will start to make that choice subconsciously every time. This leads to a compounding effect that will allow you to see stunning results as time goes on.

I need to highlight that changing your habits does take time. If you want to achieve sustainable success, not just a burst of change that fades after a brief period, you need to let time take its course. The changes you are making now can appear very small at first, but if you repeat that behavior over an extended period, these supportive habits add up to be life-changing.

James Clear in his bestselling book Atomic Habits articulated it well by saying that habits "seem to make little difference on any given day and yet the impact they deliver over the months and years can be enormous. It is only when looking back two, five, or perhaps ten years later that the value of good habits and the cost of bad ones becomes strikingly apparent". The important part of this step is to realize that you are developing habits that support a healthy future, which means they must be given time to compound into big differences.

Many people are experts at negative compounding, where small negative choices repeated over vast periods of time add up to a net negative. Poor habit development leads them to get in the way of their ability to achieve their goals. Negative compounding can be just as powerful as its positive counterpart but in the opposite direction. To stop compounding negative habits, focus on turning those habits into positive ones.

Positive compounding uses a similar theory to achieve the opposite effect. It involves the introduction of tiny, one percent difference changes in daily behaviors that get amplified over time. In positive compounding, "things add up.

You learn one skill. Then another. You finish one project. Then another. Over time, your accomplishments add up to form an impressive feat" (Foroux, n.d., para. 14). The trick is not to get caught up in failing to see immediate results in 30, 60, or even 90 days, reverting back to poor choices, and losing your momentum. Real compounding can take much longer to get going, but it is worth it for the incredible success you can use it to achieve. When setting your long-term goals, think about those that can be accomplished over no less than five years. That may seem like a very long time, but if you want results that last, you need to be thinking long term. That way, even if introducing the habit takes you 90 days, the initial time to implement that habit will be minuscule compared to the positive impact over the next 1800 days or more. The problem that many people face is that they try and take drastic leaps in a short period. Remember, you only need to make incremental changes and let them build and this will offer a life-time change and impact, not just a short-term solution.

Incremental Introduction

It is an essential stage of 'The Habit Switch' to break down the process of how to put a new habit into action, and this is by introducing it incrementally as you would now expect. To provide you with a clear example, let us assume that you currently rise at 7:00 AM, but you would like to get up at 6:20 AM so that you can add in an extra 30 minutes of reading in your day. Merely setting the alarm for 6:20 AM and trying to change your schedule with no build-up preparation is likely to get you hitting the snooze button, which could lead to you accidentally sleeping in even later than your usual time. If you take the time to wake up five minutes earlier every few days incrementally, something that takes much less willpower will easily allow you to reach 6:20 AM with minimal effort or impact on your alertness or energy levels.

I have used this example to great effect in my previous book 'Magnetic Goals'. In the example I offer the following strategy;

Start by initially setting your alarm five minutes earlier every third day, six days per week, with Sunday being a day when you can sleep in. The schedule shows how a small change every three days would play out, allowing you five minutes to get out of bed and perhaps make a cup of tea before beginning to read.

Week 1, Mon/Tues/Weds: 6:55 AM alarm, no reading at this stage.

Week 1, Thurs/Fri/Sat: Alarm is wound back by 5 minutes to 6:50 AM. Still no reading at this stage.

Week 2, Mon/Tues/Weds: 6:45 AM alarm, 10 minutes of reading commences

Week 2, Thurs/Fri/Sat: Alarm is brought back to 6:40 AM alarm, permitting 15 minutes of reading

Week 3, Mon/Tues/Weds: 6:35 AM alarm, 20 minutes of reading

Week 3, Thurs/Fri/Sat: Alarm is brought back to 6:30 AM alarm, permitting 25 minutes of reading

Week 4, Mon/Tues/Weds: 6:25 AM alarm, 30 minutes of reading

Week 4, Thurs/Fri/Sat: Alarm is brought back to 6:20 AM alarm, permitting you to reach you goal of 35 minutes of reading

In just 30 days, you have shifted your schedule to achieve a 6:20 AM start to your day, and you have accumulated over two hours of reading in the process. This is great, but the biggest change will now start to compound, now that you have extra time in your schedule to read.

Over one year, you will have an extra 40 minutes in your schedule, six days a week, 52 weeks a year, totaling an extra 208hrs in your schedule. This is the equivalent of adding 8 ½ additional days to your year. If you can keep this up for five years, you can achieve 1,032 extra hours or 43 days you did not have access to before. Trust me; you won't miss the 40 minutes of sleep each day in the face of the significant benefits you will receive. Being able to read hundreds of books you would have otherwise missed out on can produce amazing, substantial changes in your life and improve your skills and knowledge.

Blocking Out Temptation

Healthy habit change will help you avoid the bad habits you might otherwise engage in and develop a blind spot for the things that would have otherwise caught your eye. When you eat junk food regularly, especially sugary foods, you tend to seek them out and crave them. Once you cut down on your consumption, seeing junk food does not tempt you quite as much as it once did. For example, grocery and convenience stores tend to place sugary items like confectionary near the check-out aisle, so they catch your eye as you wait for your turn. Harmful eating habits that result in a dependency on sugar create attractions to these items and increase the likelihood you will buy one on your way out. Once you develop healthy eating habits, these items seem to all but disappear from your vision. They become much easier to ignore, to the point that I rarely notice them at all now, as they rest firmly in my blind spot.

Healthy habits aren't just limited to diet. They also involve exercise and small changes to improve your exercise schedule over time will provide huge benefits in the long run. Where most people get it wrong is by trying to do too much and make significant changes in short periods of time. By doing this, you risk burning yourself out and not having the energy you need to get your healthy, incremental exercise done each day. If you skip the slow adjustment process and dive right in, you can end up feeling sore, nauseous, develop discomfort, risk an injury, or have reduced motivation to stick to your plan. This is why the incremental approach is so valuable.

The Marketing Geniuses – Avoiding the Lure of the Diet and Fitness Fad

Top marketers at big companies are pros at guiding public opinion. Food marketing, in particular, is a large industry that makes up everything from dairy to produce junk food like chips and cookies. It is sometimes hard to settle in for a movie without first walking by the bright lights advertising the bucket of popcorn or the choc tops or even the extra-large soft drinks all reduced to a special price just for movie go'ers. Still, you know that these kinds of foods are okay as occasional treats but aren't healthy for you in the long run. While you may occasionally give into the temptation to enjoy a handful of popcorn, you know that all the butter and salt isn't doing you any favors.

The same cannot always be said for food marketing that masquerades as health tips. Unfortunately, there is a lot of conflicting advice about what you should and shouldn't be eating to stay healthy. Most people agree that having a slice of cake every day isn't a healthy choice, but opinions differ when it comes to things like meat consumption, fats, and carbs. What is healthy on one diet may be disallowed entirely on another. Keep a sharp eye out for any claims that seem to come from smart marketing rather than an honest portrayal of eating the right foods and in correct proportions.

Many companies try to dress up their products as 'healthier' alternatives to the more standard versions, and while this may technically be true, this doesn't always mean they are healthy. A slice of cake is healthier than the whole cake, but it is still packed with sugar and butter. Keep in mind that just because something is technically healthier than its alternative, that does not mean it is healthy or that you should eat it regularly. For example, light beer or low carb beer may be considered healthier than full-strength beer, but it's not nearly as good for you as water would be in the equivalent amounts, and the consumption of light beer can still lead to similar health concerns as full-strength beer if you consume too many. A product that is lower in fats or sugars than another may only be lower by a gram or two, even though they claim "lower fat" would lead most people to believe the difference is more drastic than that. Some marketing will also use various spelling variations like 'Lite Sour Cream' or use stats to confuse you; for example 20% less fat. You should then ask, 20% less fat than what? If it is 20% less fat now, what was it beforehand? It is important to always have a critical eye for marketing practices that try to capitalize on health trends so that you can identify the truly helpful advice from the fakes.

Similar technically true but misleading claims can be seen in fitness workout plans. Pay special attention to buzzwords meant to draw your attention without crossing the boundary into being misleading. To give an example of this in the exercise industry, how often have you seen the word *unsurpassed* thrown around? Would this imply that it is significantly better than the alternatives, without being misleading? Something like "unsurpassed" suggests that a program is better than all other alternatives, when in reality it may be just about the same, or even slightly worse with no official measurements comparing the two programs.

Always remain cautious and assume that if something sounds too good to be true, it just might be, especially when it comes to health and fitness trends and the growing market that is worth billions of dollars annually.

The Troubles with Trends

The health and fitness market has recently become especially profitable as more people look for healthy alternatives to their typical patterns and prioritize getting in shape. In the last decade, "there's been a 108% increase in the healthy eating and nutrition market to $276.5 billion, and a 78% increase in personalized health to $243 billion," so to call the industry booming might be an understatement (Settembre, 2018, para. 13). While helpful advice is always welcome, certain fitness trends are less about providing reliable advice and more about providing a short-term solution that will ensure their product or service with notoriety. Be wary of trends that are more focused on marketing than concrete, actionable advice.

Trends are by their very nature temporary booms, which does not speak well to their effectiveness in the long term. They tend to focus on weekly or even daily results instead of considering the importance of long-term achievements. Remember that when you are setting your habits, you want to choose behaviors that will help you see results over the journey of five years as a minimum, so make sure the advice you listen to holds up under scrutiny and isn't just a passing trend or fad that will go out of fashion in a few months.

Holiday Marketing

Every holiday celebration seems to involve food of some kind, and very little of it tends to be healthy. Marketing agencies have altered our eating habits around these events to suggest we break our good habits and eat more sugary and fatty foods. Be wary of what you are consuming on holidays and try not to let it interfere too much with maintaining your habits. Easter is usually celebrated with mass amounts of chocolate, but there is no reason why these foods must be involved in your holiday schedule. Christmas involves all kinds of unhealthy foods like heavily processed ham, cookies, pudding, and other desserts. Valentine's Day is all about chocolate, but some beautiful roses might make for a suitable substitute. Even sporting events are plagued by marketing for soft drinks, beer, hot dogs, and junk food.

You do not need to give these kinds of foods up entirely, but it does help to moderate how much of it you eat during a holiday. Do your best to stick to your healthy habits rather than falling into marketing pitfalls that encourage overindulgence and see where you can substitute healthy or non-food alternatives.

No Plan = No Direction

If you don't know what your end goal is and how you plan to get there, how can you begin to work towards it? A solid plan is imperative for success. If you want to get ahead, make a Personal Growth Development Plan that includes all the outcomes you want to achieve and what you need to do to pull off those outcomes. Brian Tracy, bestselling author and top international speaker, says that Personal Growth Development Plans largely focus on the process of setting your goals, making a plan and schedule for reaching those goals, and concentrating on the high-value goals. He encourages people to take their time to decide on what they are trying to do before they start working so they know which direction to head. Whatever your big dream or goals are, keep them in your thoughts as you commit yourself to establish and to maintain better habits. Once you know what you are trying to do, you can start planning and organizing your daily habits to support the goals you wish to achieve.

Structuring Your Day

Scheduling your habits throughout the day can be the difference between diligently keeping them and letting them fall by the wayside. Think about what you want to accomplish each day. These should be small scale changes and activities that you can repeat and turn into habits over time. Then arrange these actions into a schedule that fits with your needs and your lifestyle, creating patterns and routines you stick to nearly every day.

Routines in the morning and evening are very important, so focus on these to begin with. Morning routines help you wake up refreshed and ready to succeed over all of the day's challenges. Routines in the morning and evening "prime you for success. They help you achieve more, think clearly, and do work that matters. They keep you from stumbling through your day and make sure you get the most important things done" (Altrogge, 2019, para. 3). Evening routines help you wind down from a busy day and get enough sleep for the next day. Structuring your day around habits and routines that support your health and fitness will help you get closer to your goals each day.

G.O.A.L.S
Goals Offer Alternative Life Stories

Goal setting establishes clarity on what you need to do to develop the right habits and therefore making adjustments to your subsequent behaviors that will build your momentum. Your goals will give you a measure of control over your life that you may not have had otherwise because it can direct you towards a target or purpose instead of leaving you to just drift through life. Once you know which direction you should be going, you can take the appropriate steps to get there.

Brian Tracy also says that goals help you take notice of your progress by giving you a metric to measure them against. If you are trying to get in shape, you may get discouraged if you don't feel you are making much progress, but after assessing the situation, you may realize that while you have not yet met your goal, you have made significant progress from where you began. Knowing your finish line lets you track your progress and see the impact your small changes have made. Goals allow you to create a new path and develop brand new opportunities, life experiences, and stories. They help you become aware of the actions you need to take every day to succeed. You only need to know how to use them to their full effect.

DR. ACTION™

DR. ACTION™ is a goal-setting strategy that I developed that will help you identify the outcomes that matter most to you and get the most out of your goals. It will help walk you through the process of determining your ideal outcome and strategizing how you want to go about achieving it. This system is described in more detail in my book *Magnetic Goals*, but here is a brief overview of each component.

- **Dream Big** - Dream big and stretch yourself. Get clarity on what you want.
- **Relevant** - Make it personal and relevant to you.
- **Action** - Take immediate action and write up your big goals.
- **Coordinates** - Develop your plan and course of action steps.
- **Time** - Develop concrete time frames that are realistic for your goals.
- **Implement** - Follow through with your commitment and start.
- **Opportunity** - Be observant of opportunities that will present themselves.
- **Now** > Begin your journey now - your dreams can become a reality.

Understanding and implementing the steps of this process will help you develop goals that inspire change.

Dream Big

The first stage of goal setting is using your

imagination and visualization skills to think of the things you want to achieve. Picture your perfect future life and what that life involves. Be bold and think big, and don't get caught up in what seems realistic and what doesn't. These goals should be incredibly empowering when you think of them as achievable. They need to be able to drive you through the tough times and encourage you to push yourself, so they need to be things you have a strong attachment to that will help you remain resilient even when the road ahead seems tough. Start by simply visualizing your future and thinking of everything you want to achieve. What would your perfect house be like, your ideal family vacation and your perfect lifestyle? What do your health and fitness goals need to be to get you there? What would your ideal fitness level look like? Once you have thought of these end goals, attach a reason or purpose to each one.

Relevant

Your goals should matter to you. Whether or not they live up to others' expectations is irrelevant. You are the one being motivated by the goals, so do not let the opinions of others get in the way of pursuing what you want. If your goals are deeply personal and meaningful, you will find it easier to develop a near-obsessive focus on achieving them rather than trying to push yourself to do something you don't have any real passion for. Think about what makes certain goals relevant to you and what differentiates them from those you have no passion for. What will this goal mean to you when you achieve it? What positive impact will it have on you and perhaps friends and family that will also benefit from it being achieved? You must know the answers to these questions when you set your goals.

Relevance is also important because you will be taking actions to achieve your goals every single day. There is no day off when you are working towards success, and even the rest days are meant to help you recuperate so you can be ready to get to work again the next day. If you are going to commit yourself to repeat an action every day for months or years, you need to care about what you are doing so you can keep putting energy into your actions. Take ownership of your goals, as they need to be yours and yours alone.

Action

Once you have established your goals, the next step is to start taking action. Nothing gets done unless you start doing it. There is no time for procrastination and hesitation. Start by writing down your goals so you can easily reference them to remind yourself what you are working for. Writing down your dreams is a bit like the process of inking a tattoo; you are laying out the groundwork upon which the color of the goal tattoo will be filled in. Your lines need to be strong, so they can guide your future endeavors.

The process of writing goals helps sow the seeds of development in your subconscious. It keeps the goals at the forefront of your mind and gives you some accountability for completing the goals because you have made a contract with yourself to finish them. From this, future growth will spring. If you neglect to write your goals and allow yourself to procrastinate starting on your goals, you cannot expect anything to change. If you want to see real, measurable differences in your health and fitness, you need to take action.

Coordinates

Just like on a real map, your coordinates show you where you currently are, and the coordinates of your destination show you where you need to go. They are the plan that will take you from one place to the other. If you start with a well-thought-out plan, you will not stumble as you proceed through the path to success.

Without a plan, you cannot know where you are headed, and so you will not know where you are going to end up. You could end up veering off course or, worse, completely stagnating and giving up on your goals. You want to avoid taking this risk, so make sure your plan contains actionable steps you can use to keep moving forward. Making a plan and establishing your coordinates means your mind will subconsciously begin to work through the steps and make choices that bring you closer to making your dreams become a reality.

Time

Great goals have time limits that are specific and realistic while still encouraging you to always keep making progress. Your mind will do a lot of the heavy lifting for you for this step, as it has a good idea of how long it will realistically take you to do something. Once set, the deadline will remain in the back of your mind, subconsciously pushing you to make sure you are getting everything done that you need to each day.

Once you have an overarching timeline, you can break down each step of your goal plan into its own time frame. Will a certain action take you a month, or is it something that you could reasonably get done in a week? Can you complete the first stage of your journey in a year? These questions help you set the pace of your journey and keep you on track for finishing on time.

Allocating a certain amount of time to each goal helps you prioritize the actions you need to take to achieve it. If you set no time limit on finishing reading a book, it may sit unread for months. If you tell yourself, you must finish it in three weeks; you are more likely to pick up the book every time your eyes pass over it. On many occasions, one goal's completion will lead right into the next. To keep on track, complete your 12-month goals so you can move closer to your two years goals, and so on.

Your time frame also gives you a good idea of the parameters you have and provides you with a sense of accountability for completing your goals on time. As you stay on track and draw closer to the deadline, you can prepare to celebrate your accomplishments.

Implement

The implementation phase is when all of your dreaming and planning comes to a head. Many people do not make it to the implementation phase. They spend all their time thinking about what their life could be like, but they never step up and put their goal plans into practice. If you want to achieve your goals, the magic begins here. Just starting to implement your plan lets you kickstart your motivation and gets you on track. If you can manage to take that first step and make the commitment to following through on your plans, you will have a huge chance of actually reaching your goals so long as you stay true to the course. Simply start your journey and follow the path you have made for yourself, and the rest will come easily to you.

241

Opportunity

Opportunities are always around us, and frequently we let them pass by without even noticing their presence. It is up to you to recognize them and take advantage of them when they appear. If you don't make the most out of your opportunities when they arise, they are often passed on to others, while you remain exactly where you began.

The opportunity component of DR. ACTION™ is all about awareness. Learn to recognize the signs of an opportunity so you can make the most of it. You can make this process easier by reviewing your goals regularly, which tunes your mind into things that will help you get ahead and accomplish your objectives. When an opportunity does arrive, take action. If you need to make a phone call, send an email, or get in touch with someone for a follow-up conversation, do so as soon as possible. Don't let the task sit around for a few days while you debate whether or not to do it. If you procrastinate on an amazing opportunity, you just might find that it is no longer available when you finally get around to it.

Now

The final step of the DR. ACTION™ process is to act now, not later. You've completed all the preliminary work you need to get to this point. It is the time to put all of your planning into action right now. Let your motivation and momentum carry you forward and get off on the right foot. You will need a significant personal commitment, clear daily structure, a good plan, courage, and the ability to tackle your hesitations with ruthless perseverance, but so long as you keep taking action, you can achieve your goals.

Chapter 3

STOP>REVIEW>PIVOT and POWER

Progress reports allow businesses to see how much work and improvement a person or team has made on a project. They are essential for ensuring deadlines are being met, and progress is being made. But what if you could use a progress report to review your situation in regards to your health and fitness? I designed the *STOP>REVIEW>PIVOT* and *POWER* system so that my clients have an opportunity to review and reflect on where they currently are and change direction if their current course is not taking them where they need to go. It also supplies its users with the power to build up their momentum and make a real impact on their lives. With this system, you can develop an honest assessment of your current status and understand what needs to be changed in order to achieve success.

The system is made up of four components, each of which has a unique purpose that helps you self-evaluate. The steps will help you identify if your current habits are progressing your chances to achieve a healthy lifestyle, or if your habits are hindering the opportunity to obtain a suitable balance of your fitness level and a healthy diet. By placing the habits you engage in every day under the microscope, you can get a good sense of what's working and what's holding you back that may otherwise have been left unnoticed.

Each step will be explained in more detail, but first, I want to give a brief explanation of what the steps of the system do.

The first step, **STOP**, asks you to pause and consider the exact moment you are in right now. Don't think about where you were a year ago, and don't count anything you plan on doing in the future. Just focus on the here and now and pinpoint if, at this very moment, your current daily habits are taking you in your intended direction.

Next, **REVIEW** requires you to look at your answer and identify what is working well and separate it from what isn't. What changes would you need to implement to get back on course? Can you identify any triggers that have a history of causing you to lapse in your determination and undo all the progress you have made so far and will make in the future?

PIVOT is the process of beginning to implement the changes you have identified during your review. This may be only a marginal change of direction or an increase in your commitment to your goals, or it may involve an entire overhaul of your plan and new goals you wish to achieve. In nearly all circumstances, you will still use the process of introducing mini habits to make these new changes.

In the final stage, **POWER**, your renewed commitment and clarity will give you purpose. This provides you with the energy you need to push forward knowing you have conducted a thorough review, you have the right action plan in place, and you are now in the perfect position to achieve your fitness, diet, and overall health goals.

STOP - Where Do You Sit Right Now on a Scale of One to 10?

It can be a challenge to grade your current performance in relation to your goals to pinpoint precisely how you are tracking. To help you, I want to walk you through the actionable steps so you can conduct your very own performance review with the *STOP>REVIEW>PIVOT* and *POWER* system.

The first step is taking time to reflect and giving yourself a grade on your current position. You can fill out the questions as I guide you through the process, and this is all about taking *ACTION* in the moment. So, take out a notebook and a pen or pencil and answer the following questions with either of three options being yes, no, or occasionally. Your answers will provide you with just a basic level of your current condition, but you can refer back to them at any future point as they form a great reference point you can continue from.

Exercise/Fitness:

1. Do you exercise for a minimum of 30 minutes a day, five days per week?

2. When exercising, do you reach a point of perspiration in at least two of your sessions each week?

3. Do you have time in the day specifically set aside to exercise?

4. Do you find ways to make exercise fun and participate in activities you enjoy?

5. Do you always introduce new fitness habits incrementally into your schedule because you view these new habits from a long-term perspective?

6. Are you conscious of activities considered to be high impact and the risk associated with these activities on your joints as you age? For example, swimming, golf, yoga, and cycling are low impact activities. Basketball, netball, hockey, and running on hard surfaces are considered high impact activities.

Diet/Nutrition:

1. Do you eat a minimum or the equivalent of two handfuls of fresh vegetables and two handfuls of fruit (if cut up into pieces) each day?

2. Do you drink a minimum of two litres of water each day?

3. Do you make a conscious effort to ensure that your breakfast does not contain high levels of fats, high levels of sugars, or more than a cup of dairy products like milk and cheese?

4. Do you understand that marketing can significantly influence you and condition you to eat the wrong foods, and therefore stay away from gimmick "diet fads"?

5. Are you committed to restricting too much snacking throughout the day, particularly with items full of sugar and preservatives?

6. Are you always health-conscious when doing your shopping and do you rotate your nutrition sources, so you are not eating the same foods day in and day out?

Now, add up your score based on your answers. Each *YES* is worth five points, each *OCCASIONALLY* is worth three points, and each **NO** is worth one point. Compare your total score to the following score summaries.

Summarizing your score

A combined score between **12 and 25** indicates there are numerous negative habits that will need to be addressed and adjusted across your diet and exercise patterns. Don't get disheartened; this is not about negative judgment. Instead, it is about self-reflection at this very moment and taking this fantastic opportunity to identify some simple but effective changes you can implement in the form of mini habits that will help you bring up your score. Importantly, you are absolutely on the right track, and I commend you for this. You have taken the right action by reading The Habit Switch, and you are ready to commit to a lifelong change. As you continue to read and implement your plan for improving your health and fitness, stop and take action when required. Start to implement healthy habits into your daily routine that will replace some of the less supportive ones you may still use. A combined score of **26 to 45** suggests you have identified some areas of potential improvement. Adding a few extra mini habits to your schedule to bolster your current diet and exercise plans will help you further improve your score. You have a firm grasp on the basics of keeping yourself healthy, but there are still a few ways in which you can significantly improve your long-term health and well-being with additional incremental changes.

A combined score between **46 and 60** indicates that you are tracking very well across your health and fitness. You are likely engaging in mini habits already that help to keep your momentum moving towards your goals. Even if you score high on this preliminary questionnaire, you have likely noticed there are some areas you can continue to improve in. Remember, the above questions will provide a baseline feel for your current habits and that they do not represent all the things you could be doing to get and stay healthy. We will dive deeper into other areas of exercise and diet that will enable you to take your health and fitness to another level later in the book.

At this point, the initial step of **_STOP_** helps you identify some of the amazing benefits of a healthy lifestyle and where these benefits can come into play in your own life. These include:

- Improving your self-esteem and self-confidence
- Improving your clarity of mind, memory, and focus
- Reducing the risk of many diseases including cardiovascular disease, stroke, and diabetes

- Improving your flexibility, muscle strength, and range of movement
- Helping you maintain balance and coordination as you age
- Significantly reducing the onset of osteoporosis and lessening the chances of bone fractures
- Improving your ability and speed for recovering from various illnesses
- Reducing the symptoms of stress, anxiety, and depression, subsequently improving your sense of well-being and happiness

Stopping and making an assessment of where your current habits are steering you allows you to keep ahead of the pack on your fitness journey and get closer to achieving all of these benefits and more.

REVIEW - Reflection and Observation

A review of your plan needs to be an ongoing process that you regularly conduct so you can determine if you are moving in the right direction. You may require some course correction, and it can be helpful when you first commence to review yourself initially after one month, then three months, and then every six months after that. Part of this focus for reviewing your goals is to ensure you are preparing yourself adequately to achieve your desired outcomes, and also that you still want to pursue the goals you have chosen.

Start to think about the decisions that you have made up to this point. Which ones have benefitted your progress, and which ones have hindered it? Being able to review your past choices and current habits gives you insight into what is working and what isn't so that you can more effectively target the areas in need of improvement.

Reflection is helpful in many fields, not just fitness. It allows us to recognize our blind spots and fix them where we can. It is an opportunity for inward reflection, but not one for being overly critical of yourself. This is because you are currently in a transitionary period of change, and change takes time. It is unfair to expect yourself to be much farther than you are without giving yourself the proper time to enact the change you want to see. If your focus on your goals has slipped, think about why this may have happened and what you can do to get it back on track, not on berating yourself.

In goal setting, there is a lot of temptation always to look forward and never look back. You are focused on what you should do next and how it will help you achieve your goals. But taking the time to look backwards and evaluate your performance to date can be helpful too. You want to always keep your goals in mind, but you need to celebrate and appreciate what you have achieved on your journey. Past mistakes and successes both need to be acknowledged as they will assist in changing or reinforcing the decisions that initially led to them.

During the Review stage, make sure to always remain honest with yourself and remember that reflection is a wonderful learning opportunity. Your improvement may be impacted, and you will never be able to make the appropriate changes if you don't give yourself a genuine review. You do not need to be overly critical, but you should consider what you could have done differently in a given situation. Only an honest view will show how you can improve.

An Example Review

If you are still a little unsure of what an effective review looks like, use the following example. You can adjust the questions to fit your own goals more specifically if needed.

My Health Review (conducted after one month): Date:

1. The new supportive habits I have introduced since my last review are:
2. The habit(s) that I have had difficulty implementing since my previous review have been:
3. Out of 10, how would I honestly rate my current progress?   /10
4. If my rating is under 6/10, what will I need to do to lift my rating to an 8/10?
5. If I rated yourself higher than a 6/10, what habits would I need to implement to score 10/10?
6. Do I still feel that my clarity and focus are always aligned to my ideal desired outcomes?
7. What have been my biggest challenges or roadblocks since the previous review?
8. If I identified roadblocks or particular challenges with introducing my supportive mini habits,

what do I need to do to 'pivot' and change direction?

9. What are the top five mini habit goals that I wish to achieve prior to my next review?

10.   What is my plan to incrementally introduce these habits with a long-term view? That is, if these habits were to be part of my day for the next five years, how would I introduce the habit slowly, over a 60-90 day period?

The ability to give yourself an honest review is an invaluable skill, but not one that comes easily to everyone. If you need further guidance on the process, try making use of the following resources:

- *La Trobe University's (Australia) "Reflective Practice in Health" for a step-by-step guide to reflection*
- *The Telegraph's "Six Daily Decisions that can Make or Break Your Health" for more information about differentiating between good and bad decisions*

PIVOT - A Change of Direction

You know what's working and what's not. Now it's time to take that knowledge and implement it. There are two possible results from the Review process. The first is that you may find that you are on track to complete your goals and you do not have to make changes to your approach after all, or the changes you need to make are very minimal. In this case, proceed with the groundwork you have laid down, making the small adjustments and additions you have identified. With perseverance and time, you will reach your health and fitness goals. Don't attempt to tweak things if your only goal is speeding up the process. As we have discussed, real change takes time and trying to rush it can lead you to unfortunate side-effects.

The other possible result from the Review process is that you have identified a few or more areas that would benefit from alterations, additions, and replacements for negative habits that are impeding your progress. This result tends to be more common as we slip back into old behavior patterns and our focus wavers on our goals. It is nothing to be ashamed of, especially if you are just starting out on making serious improvements to your health. So long as you can rebound from it, this can actually be a result that helps reinvigorate you. It is always better to identify these less than helpful habits sooner rather than later. The good news is that now that you have identified the problem, you can take the proper steps to correct it.

Habit Pivoting

Pivoting your habits is the process of replacing negative habits with positive ones. If you have decided that a particular habit is no longer helping you reach your goals, swap it out for one that will. This can be as simple as increasing 20 minutes of daily exercise to 30 minutes, or it could mean something more involved, like starting a new exercise routine entirely.

If you need to make significant changes, make sure you are implementing them incrementally. Start with small intervals of exercise and dietary changes and slowly transition to new habits over time. Evaluate the direction of your new plan to decide how quickly new habits should be implemented and what your expected results will be.

Goal Pivoting

In some cases, you may find that your current

goals no longer resonate with you, and you need to change your goals themselves. This can be a tough call to make, but if it is necessary, then you are better off pivoting than trying to pursue something you no longer feel passionate about. Taking steps to make a change happen when you notice one coming lets you decide the direction you will pivot and gives you agency. If you wait too long, often life has a way of making the change without your input and taking you along for the ride (Sreenivasan, 2017, para. 3). Take the opportunity to sit and write down your new desired outcomes so you can repeat the goal-setting process. When you have successfully shifted your goals, you can begin deciding on the new habit plan for achieving the outcomes you have chosen to pursue.

POWER - A Renewed and Committed Focus for Your Health

The final part of the system is to power onwards! All the revisions you have made to your plan should leave you feeling more committed than ever before. With the renewed energy and focus you are feeling, you can keep pushing forward and using your mini habits to your advantage.

Remember that your review process represents a commitment to yourself. If you have identified areas in need of change, you have to follow through and make those changes. Keep the daily reminders of your habits and goals easily visible, so you stick to them. Make yourself a well-structured schedule you can follow that keeps you accountable for completing all of your habits each day.

An ongoing investment in your health is critical for all other fields of self-improvement. You spend so much of your time trying to benefit others. Take some time to improve yourself and make sure your body is always running at peak performance. After all, you need a healthy, reliable body to carry you to achieve all of your goal. That is why you must take your new habits and goals seriously and fully commit yourself to them.

Completing a self-review every 3 – 6 months is a minimal time commitment. Set aside just one hour every three to six months so you can work through the review process, adjust the direction you are moving, and then power forward to achieve success.

Confidence Builders - The 1 % Changes

Momentum and change build confidence. We need to view our progress as motivational and let it carry us through to future successes. When you really care about what you are doing, every step you take will feel like its own success. These simple, one percent changes that you make every day or even every week can exponentially improve your self-esteem, especially when you learn to recognize their huge compounding impact.

Ongoing improvements always make a difference, no matter how small. If you cut candy out of your diet, even if it doesn't lead to immediate weight loss, you are still taking steps to make yourself healthier. If you expand on this change with a series of continuous improvements, you will find that in a year or two, you end up leagues ahead of where you began. It may seem unglamorous at first. We are bombarded by success stories of how people made millions overnight or lost 20 pounds in two weeks, and while these stories are alluring, they represent one in a million odds. The difference between them and your path to progress is that everyone can make a one percent change, repeated over time, without any need for luck. James Clear, author of Atomic Habits says that it may be true that getting one percent better isn't going to make headlines but there is one thing about it, though: it works". You are using the tortoise method of "slow and steady" here, not the hare, which means you avoid risks like burnout. The one percent changes you make will boost your confidence and take you ever closer to your goal.

Making a 1% Change Every Day

One percent does not seem like a lot on its own, but just like habits, it can build up into something amazing. You only need to be willing to commit yourself to make tiny improvements regularly. To become one percent better each day, you need to focus on your reasons for self-improvement, the personal gratification you feel when you improve, maintaining a long-term view, and ensuring you take action consistently. Taking action is the most crucial step because without action, you will never achieve your outcomes.

If you were to change just one thing about yourself or your actions each day, do you know how much you could achieve over time? To show the amazing change you can achieve, take the example of money. If you were to start with just $100 at the beginning of the year and you were able to increase what you have by 1% every single day, at the end of the year, you would have accumulated $3,778.34 [or] 37.7 being 8x what you had at the beginning of the year. We are used to seeing compound gains like this when it comes to money, but personal improvement works the same way. One improvement will lead to the next, and before long, you will be just so far ahead of where you once were. Even if you were to make a one percent improvement every day for 100 days, only ⅓ of a year, you would be 100% better than you were when you started. The small improvements matter as long as you keep the ball rolling and remember to take smart, beneficial actions each day.

Chapter 4

How to Switch on Your Diet Habits

You can make significant improvements to your health through your diet using the mini habit method. Small changes in what you eat and how you approach eating will help you regain control over your eating habits. Learning how to flip on the habit switch and improve your diet is a matter of altering your mindset. If you want to eat healthily, lose weight, and continue to eat foods that give you energy rather than make you lethargic and exhausted, you must break free of the constraints of your old habits and be prepared to change the way you think about dieting and the power of different food sources.

264

Are You Prepared to Switch? - How to Turn off Your Former Diet Habits

We all have a set of dietary habits that determine our approach to our nutrition. The formation of these habits can be attributed to a few different factors, many of which begin in our childhood. If you ate and were told of the great benefits of eating vegetables as a child, you are more likely to have developed a taste and an appreciation for vegetables as an adult. The opposite is also true; if you had to be convinced to finish a side of broccoli as a child, you have likely built up negative associations that get in the way of eating healthy food as an adult. In this way, our dietary habits have a massive impact as we grow from children to teenagers to adults and get to choose our meals. Some negative dietary habits, usually those that are developed later in life, are often easy to recognize and change. Those that we have carried with us since childhood, almost appear to be ingrained in our subconscious mind, making them very difficult to change.

As children, we make negative and positive associations toward all kinds of food. If you were 'forced' to eat a particular type of food that you did not enjoy, you likely resented that food and hated seeing it on your plate. It can be just small things as a child that can become the stimulus that can cause negative habits later in life.

The only way to change these habits is to change the way you approach your meals, first by recognizing the power of past and current eating habits on future ones. Remove the mindset that you can, or your children can eat what you or they want while young because positive and supportive habits begin early and you establish the right foundations that will take you through at a very early age.

If for example, you spend your 20's eating bacon "while apparently you still can," you will likely continue to eat bacon well into your 40's and 50's, when the compounding impact of cholesterol can cause heart and other cardiovascular diseases. If you always think "I'll worry about that later" in regards to eating habits, when "later" finally comes those habits will be so ingrained that they will be difficult to shake.

Everything circles back to your goals and desired outcomes. What do you want to accomplish, and what would you like to avoid? This also applies to present-day health concerns you may be currently facing, not just future ones. Maybe cardio-vascular disease runs in your family, and you are looking to buck the trend. Perhaps you have young children, and you want to have enough energy to share activities with them without being out of breath. Whatever your current and future health goals are, they matter to you, so you must be willing to embrace change and break free from old habits to achieve them.

Most importantly, you have already taken your first step towards leading a healthy and uncomplicated life by picking up this book as mentioned in the introductory. I am a firm believer that certain books have come into my life at just the right times when I needed to hear their message the most. If this is true for you too, then you know that you must take the step that 90% of the population fails to do and take action, now, to implement the suggestions outlined here. Remember, The Habit Switch is all about simplicity, maintaining common sense, and practical diet habits that are sustainable in the long term. I strongly encourage you to make use of the ideas that work best for you and stick to your plan. If this is your first book about habit change for your diet, make it your last for a minimum of 12 months. If at the end of that period you find that the suggestions are not sustainable then yes, look for alternatives, but really, give these ideas time to grow first.

I want to help you by breaking information down by simplifying the steps as much as possible. My background as a teacher has provided me with the ability to break information down into smaller and more manageable steps that have been a proven method for success. Make your personal promise to 'switch' your current habits into those that will significantly improve your health for the long term.

Why a switch can add years to your life

Sticking to healthy habits will allow you to spend more time doing the activities you enjoy. In fact, some healthy habits can even add years onto your lifespan, giving you incredible amounts of extra time to get more done. A recent Harvard University study found that you can increase your life expectancy by over a decade if you follow certain healthy habits. The five habits identified in the study are:

1. Not smoking;

2. Having a body mass index between 18.5 and 25;

3. Taking at least 30 minutes of moderate exercise a day;

4. Having no more than one 150 mL glass of wine a day for women, or two for men. Personally, I think water is best anyway!

5. Having a diet rich in items such as fruit, vegetables and whole grains and low in red meat, saturated fats and sugar.

(Harvard University, 2018, para. 7)

These small changes build up into a tremendous impact on your overall health.

Most of the habits in the study are common sense suggestions, and many are relatively easy to implement in to your life style. The power of "mini things" is readily apparent here. It does not take a lot to have a big impact on your fitness; it only takes many small things combined over time. Regarding the consumption of no more than 150 mL of alcohol each day, I suggest limiting alcohol whenever possible. The problem for alcohol with many people is that it encourages snacking on cheese, crackers, or other high-fat food while they drink. This introduces unnecessary excess calories that could be avoided just by avoiding alcohol as often as you can.

Sustainable Diets are not Complicated!

In this section, I want to turn what may at times, feel complicated and overwhelming into easy to process information. I believe an effective diet must be easily understandable so that you know what you should be doing, and you have everything you need to succeed. Back when I was in school, I found some classes challenging because of the way the material was taught. It was assumed I knew certain prerequisite information, but this was incorrect. Some teachers tended to assume I was learning what was being taught, but I was missing important information and had to work twice as hard to catch-up. This is precisely what I want to avoid with my own teaching style as I walk you through developing your healthy habit plan. You should be able to have a firm grasp on the information being presented to you without risk of complex topics that leave you behind, so I have simplified my lesson plan. Get ready for a fast-track lesson on how to make a change to a healthy diet uncomplicated!

There are many different diets that are currently popular. I do not believe there is much value in comparing the pros and cons of each, as I want to focus more on giving you a brief overview of these diets. This is so you can see just how confusing it is for people without a background in anatomy, physiology, and nutrition to determine what is suitable and useful and what is just plain ludicrous. I do have my personal opinions about each of these diets, but as you continue to read about my belief systems for leading a healthy life through diet and exercise and the right foods to be eating, you can start to see where some of these trendy diets falter, especially when viewed as potential long-term solutions. Again, I'm not here to criticize and dissect the various diets that are available, instead show you how there can be contradictory diet information just across these 6 current popular diets.

The Paleo Diet

The paleo diet, as the name suggests, encourages people to eat in a way similar to their ancestors. This means cutting out processed foods, sugar, and grains. Essentially, you limit your diet to veggies, meat, fruit and nuts. Underpinning these dietary restrictions is the theory that the modern Western diet, full of dairy, grains, and processed foods, is responsible for the high rates of many diseases. Paleo tries to cut down on the number of carbohydrates in your diet in an attempt to keep these diseases at bay and encourage weight loss. According to the diet, "the fewer number of carbohydrates in your system leads to a decreased amount of glucose. So your system will then begin to use fat as its fuel source" (NutritionED, n.d., para. 2). Theoretically, by restricting carbs, you encourage your body to burn fat instead.

Plant-based or vegan diet

The vegan diet and other plant-based diets limit the foods in the diet to only those that come from plants, such as fruits, vegetables, legumes, and plant-based meat and dairy alternatives. It is an extension of the vegetarian diet that excludes animal products as well as meat. Proponents of using veganism for weight loss say it works "because its very low fat and high fiber content may make you feel fuller for longer"

(Bjarnadottir, 2019, para. 3). This is an opposite approach to many low-carb diets, which typically have higher fats, lower fiber, and almost always include meat products. Many people engage in plant-based diets for moral reasons rather than purely weight loss ones, though some dieters have simply chosen to eat animal product-free because they believe in the health benefits.

The Atkins Diet

The Atkins diet is a type of low-carb diet that emphasizes both proteins and fats, which it suggests are meant to keep your fuller for longer periods of time. Proponents of the diet "insist that you can lose weight by eating as much protein and fat as you like, as long as you avoid carbs" (Bjarnadottir, 2019, para. 7). Its main goal is weight loss. The diet is split into four phases, each of which has different requirements for how much of your diet is made up of carbs, proteins, and fat. The Atkins diet also claims that "obesity and related health problems, such as type 2 diabetes and heart disease, are the fault of the typical low-fat, high-carbohydrate American diet" (Mayo Clinic Staff, 2017, para. 6). People who follow the diet increase their fat intake rather than cutting down on it, and instead focus on limiting carbs.

Intermittent Fasting

Intermittent fasting is a process of eating during certain hours and fasting during others. It does not suggest avoiding any particular types of food; instead, it provides guidelines for when you should be eating. There are many different eating patterns involved in intermittent fasting, each one suggesting different intervals of time between meals and sometimes different times of day when it is more optimal to fast or eat. By nature, it requires you to skip meals throughout the day. Sometimes this can become more extreme periods of time, as "common intermittent fasting methods involve daily 16-hour fasts or fasting for 24 hours, twice per week" (Gunnars, 2018, para. 2). The fasting is meant to reduce your overall caloric intake, which in turn leads to weight loss.

The Keto Diet

The keto diet is a more extreme version of low-carb diets like Atkins. It suggests eliminating nearly all carbohydrates from your diet and supplementing them with higher fat intake. This effectively removes an entire macronutrient from your meals. Supporters of the diet say it "lowers blood sugar and insulin levels, and shifts the body's metabolism away from carbs and towards fat and ketones," which act as alternative energy sources (Mawer, 2018, para. 3). A successful keto diet attempt involves entering a state known as ketosis, where your body shifts to these alternative fuels and burns stored fat. Keto diet plans are full of high-fat foods like red meat, nuts, eggs, and even the fairly frequent incorporation of bacon, which is typically viewed as a cause of weight gain, not the solution to it.

The TLC Diet
The TLC diet does not stand for tender loving care, as the typical use of the acronym would have you believe. Instead, it is short for Therapeutic Lifestyle Changes. It suggests making food selections that benefit your heart health. Typical distribution of nutrients on the diet encourages dieters to get "50-60% of their daily calories from

carbs, 24-35% from fat, and 15% from protein" (Sass, 2019, para. 2). The TLC standard diet includes plenty of vegetables, fruit, whole grains, nuts, and low fat or nonfat dairy. It also allows for low-fat protein selections like fish and skin-off poultry. It is designed primarily for keeping cholesterol low, though it is believed to have weight loss benefits as well.

Eating for sustainability

Now that you have a brief background on these six dieting styles, let me outline what an easy and sustainable diet should consist of. We will delve into a few different areas, but my aim is to keep things simplified. Remember, there is no miraculous fix, no silver bullet that will let you shed dozens of pounds in no time without some hidden drawback. Your health is predominantly determined by ensuring you have a high intake of the right foods and nutrients rather than eliminating the bad foods in your diet. If you focus on eating the right food sources, you won't have to worry about eating the wrong things. Your nutritional needs need to be met in the most simplified, functional, and practical way possible.

Before starting on any diet, ask yourself, is this diet sustainable for 10 years? If not, you may want to reconsider if it will help you achieve your long-term health goals.

The Eight Tips to Develop a Long-Term Healthy Habit Plan for Your Diet

Note that my intention in this section is not to dive deep into the specifics and design a healthy meal chart for breakfast, lunch, and dinner, nor am I giving you specific recipes you must follow with no wiggle room. Your meal plan needs are unique to you as an individual, and this level of meal planning may require the aid of a dietician or nutritionist to assist you over the course of several sessions. My aim is to provide a guideline, dispel some confusion, bring things into clear focus, and allow you to make healthy choices moving forward that you can implement with mini habits. This is the goal of my eight key tips to mastering healthy diet habits.

Healthy Tip 1
Mix it up!

All the different kinds of food we eat have different types and combinations of nutrients, vitamins, and minerals. There is no one food or tablet supplement that can supply us with all the nutrients we need to live a full and happy life, and your diet should reflect this. For example, bananas are high in vitamin C, vitamin B, and potassium, but they contain no vitamin E or magnesium. Almonds provide us with vitamin E and magnesium but no vitamin C or potassium. To fulfill all of your body's needs, you need to incorporate many different foods into your meals. Variety is imperative in any diet, and not just for health reasons. Eating a wide variety of foods helps you put more care into what you are eating and mix up your diet, which can lead you to try foods you've never had before and discover a new love for something you wouldn't have otherwise tried. Eating the same foods every week makes mealtime boring and makes it easy to stop paying attention to what you are putting in your body, especially if every week you are eating something that is not so healthy for you.

I would suggest you try adjusting your eating habits based on the current season, selecting produce that is at its freshest and making meals that compliment them. This means eating foods like watermelon, cucumbers, avocado, tomatoes, and other hydrating produce in summer, while winter diets are composed of foods such as stews, grains, nuts, carrots beans etc. You may already naturally be pulled towards these types of meals as the seasons change. Eating based on what is in season is a great way to create variety in your diet with the added benefit that they may be cheaper as they are in more abundance at that time of the year. Currently, most produce is available seasonally due to grocery stores' ability to stock foods from other parts of the world and store them for longer periods, but trying to pick up some locally grown produce at a local fruit and veg store.

Healthy Tip 2
Hydration

We all need water. But are you getting as much of it as you should be? Drinking enough water can help you cut down on how much you are eating and promote healthier eating habits and hydration. Drinking more water leaves less room for craving sugary drinks like soda and sweetened juices. Water is a natural source of hydration for your body, and it helps in so many ways. There is a reason you can only survive for a few days without any water because every cell, tissue, and organ in your body needs water to function at peak efficiency and if you are dehydrated, this can interfere with your body's ability to function. If you need help drinking more water, keeping a bottle of water nearby to encourage you to take a sip more often. You can add a slice of lemon or lime to mix up the flavor if you get tired of plain water. Small adjustments like these can go a long way in increasing how much water you drink each day.

Healthy Tip 3
Fiber is the natural chimney sweep!

Fiber helps your body function as it should. It keeps your digestive system regular, and a healthy supply of it prevents a variety of health problems from occurring. Fiber is found only in plant foods such as whole-grain cereals and breads, beans, peas, and many other fruits and vegetables. These plants have different types of fiber, so it is important to eat many different kinds so that your body has access to everything it needs for regular bowel function, reduced symptoms of chronic constipation, and potentially lower the risk for heart diseases and some cancers.

A good supply of fiber also helps the bacteria in your gut function properly. Bacteria is typically seen as a bad thing, but the bacteria that reside in your stomach are 'good' bacteria, the same kind that are targeted by probiotics and, as it turns out, high fiber diets. Your gut bacteria "are crucial for various aspects of your health, including weight, blood sugar control, immune function and even brain function" (Gunnars, 2018, para. 20). These bacteria can break down and thrive off the fiber in your diet, so make sure you are eating plenty to keep these functions in top shape.

Healthy Tip 4
Some Fats Can Clog Up Your Pipes

Despite the recent popularity of fats in certain diets, there are still many fats you should limit in your diet. Not all fats are equal, and from my experience and education, some are worse for your body than others. Fats and oils are in many snacks that we might not otherwise think of as fatty, like buttery crackers and anything fried. Some foods and food groups contain higher fats than others. Many foods in the dietary protein group, which contains meat, fish, poultry, eggs, beans, and nuts, are high in fats. However, this does not mean you must cut out all protein from your diet. Knowing the difference between the types of fats will help you make smart protein choices. To keep things as simple as possible, here is a brief breakdown of the different fats and what role they should play in your diet.

Saturated fats should be limited. They are primarily found in foods like red meat and milk products, as well as anything made with these products. The main concern with eating saturated fat is the buildup of cholesterol in your body. Your liver contains cholesterol receptors that break cholesterol down, but "eating too much saturated fat stops the receptors from working so well, so cholesterol builds up in the blood" (Heart UK, n.d., para. 6). This can lead to health conditions like a heart attack or stroke if not properly moderated. If you are looking to decrease saturated fats in your diet, you should pay careful attention to the fats section of ingredient labels. You can also choose lean meats like chicken, turkey, and fish instead of red meat for most of your meals. Making smart choices about how often you eat saturated fats can save you trouble in the long run.

Monounsaturated and *polyunsaturated* fats are generally seen as the less harmful counterparts to saturated fats. Monounsaturated fats are often found in things like olive oil and canola oil, while most other vegetable oils, nuts, and high-fat fish are good sources of polyunsaturated fat. While all fat should only be consumed in moderation, "eating moderate amounts of polyunsaturated (and monounsaturated) fat in place of saturated and trans fats can benefit your health" (A.D.A.M., 2018, para. 2). You need some fat in your diet, so it is best to stick to the healthier varieties.

Fats, despite their potential negative impacts, play a beneficial role in the body as well. They supply energy and essential fatty acids your body needs to function. They also help your body absorb fat-soluble vitamins A, D, E, and K. I suggest that rather than adopting a low-fat diet or aiming for no fat at all, it is important to focus on eating those beneficial 'good' fats like polyunsaturated fats and limiting harmful saturated fats. However, many people continue to have a diet high in saturated fat mainly due to a lack of knowledge in the food science area, the perceived cost of cheap takeout compared to cooking at home, and convenience. Knowing how to choose healthier fats will help you lead a healthier life.

Healthy Tip 5
Maintaining a Healthy Weight

People of all ages need to be a healthy weight. Our fitness levels are a product of the choices we make, which means that with the right choices, it is entirely possible to maintain a healthy weight. Many people use body mass index (BMI) to see if their weight is healthy for their size, but remember that your ideal weight can depend on several factors, including your height, age and sex. People who are overweight increase their risk for health conditions like high blood pressure, heart disease, diabetes, and breathing problems. Maintaining a healthy weight also means not undereating or dieting excessively either, as you need good nutrition and the energy from eating enough calories to keep yourself active and healthy.

Weight loss is greatly benefitted by physical activity along with a combination of consuming the right food in your diet. Aerobic exercises, such as walking, running, swimming, skipping, and high-intensity sports like soccer or basketball all help burn fat and calories. Staying active is an important part of any weight loss routine.

Healthy Tip 6
Consume Plenty of Vegetables, Fruits, and Grains

Fruits, vegetables, and grain products are key parts of a balanced diet. They provide important vitamins, minerals, complex carbohydrates in the form of starch and dietary fiber, and other substances that are necessary for a healthy life. They are also typically naturally low in fat, so long as they are prepared, cooked and served without too many additions.

I would encourage you to eat as many vegetables as you desire. Avoid deep-frying them or using additives like oils, sauces, or cheeses, but so long as you are sticking primarily to vegetables you can, for the most part, eat as you please.

When eating grains, be sure to choose healthier varieties like whole wheat and ancient grains. White bread and other products made with refined white flour can have added sugars that get in the way of the benefits of whole grains.

Healthy Tip 7
Avoid Consuming Too Much Sugar and Salt

You likely already know to avoid added sugars and sweeteners, but too much sugar from natural sources can be a problem too. Sugars and starches occur naturally in foods that are otherwise nutrient-rich, including fruits, some vegetables, milk, beans, breads, cereals, and other grains. Sugars are simple carbohydrates, while other dietary carbs like starch and fiber are complex carbohydrates. During digestion, all carbs except fiber break down into sugars, which means the body cannot tell the difference between added sugars and those that occur naturally. As a result, you should be wary of the amount of sugar you are eating, even from natural sources like fruits and grains. Sugars should be used in moderation by most healthy people and only sparingly by those with low-calorie needs.

Sodium chloride, or salt, also occurs naturally in foods as well as being an additive. Whether you are eating foods already high in salt or seasoning your meals with a pinch of table salt, keep an eye on how much sodium you are consuming. Of course, salt is not all bad. In the body, it plays an essential role in the regulation of fluids and blood pressure. But too much of it can lead to health concerns. People at risk of high blood pressure can lower their risk by limiting the amount of salt they eat, so get rid of the salt and pepper shakers!

Healthy Tip 8
Choose a Low Cholesterol Diet

Your body is capable of producing the cholesterol it needs. Cholesterol can also be obtained through dietary sources, typically animal products. These include egg yolks, meat and organ meats like liver especially, fish, poultry, and milk products that can be high in fat. Choosing foods with less cholesterol will help you keep your blood pressure and blood cholesterol at healthy levels.

A side note for vegetarian diets....

Many people across the world eat vegetarian diets as a result of their culture, beliefs, or individual health needs. Some vegetarians eat milk products and eggs, and as a whole, they are still able to enjoy excellent health without meat in their diet. You can get enough protein on a vegetarian diet so long as the variety and amount of protein-heavy meat alternatives consumed are adequate. If you pursue a vegetarian diet, there are still quite a few sources of protein available to you. These include eggs and dairy, as well as other non-animal products like nuts, peanut butter, legumes, soymilk, and tofu (American Academy of Family Physicians, 2019, para. 10). Still, meat, fish and poultry are major contributors of iron, zinc, and vitamin B in most diets, so vegetarians should pay special attention to getting these nutrients from sources compliant with their dieting habits. As previously mentioned, vegan diets are plant-based and contain no animal products. Because of this, it can be trickier to ensure your body is getting all of the necessary nutrients. One compound to keep in mind is vitamin B12 because it only comes from animal products. This vitamin is essential for the production of red blood cells as it does help to maintain healthy nerves and a healthy brain. Vegans must supplement their diets with other sources of B12. Additionally, vegan diets, particularly for children, require additional sources of vitamin D and calcium, which most people get from milk products.

High-quality input = High-quality output

What you put into your body defines what you get out of it. The food you eat provides the energy and nutrients that help your body function optimally and make sure you are always at your best. Nutrients from our diets also act as the building blocks of cell repair and injury prevention. Eating the right foods can help you in so many ways as they help boost your energy level, assist with protecting against some cancers, aide in concentration and make you feel happier and become more resilient to stress. The foods we choose to eat now will have long-term consequences on our health as we age. It is up to you to decide whether those consequences will be positive or negative. Again, we see the compounding impact of small behaviors over an extended period. If you make sure to eat well every day, you will see amazing returns on health, weight loss, and energy levels.

Practical Steps to Implement Your Habit Switch

Now that we have covered many areas of healthy food sources, it is time to look at the practical steps to implement the suggestions into your daily life. As we have already discussed, the basis of your new healthy change must come from small habits built incrementally into your life. This will lead to your behaviors changing when the new habits become automatic and replace any pre-existing negative habits. Just as weight gain can be a product of small changes, so too can weight loss.

We will begin our practical steps for a habit

switch with the very basics and continue to build from there.

Practical Step 1

The 72-hour test and trial

Sit down and think carefully about which dietary goals you can achieve within three days from now. Why just three days? We want to initially focus on the small changes we can implement and review in 72 hours so you can know if they are effective. We will move on to setting longer-term goals later, but first, just focus on the small steps, not the lifetime benefits you will see if you keep taking them. Get some initial wins on the board, build your foundation for change, and encourage confidence.

As a reminder, building habits incrementally requires the following key elements:

1. Changes must be small and incremental with a long-term mindset.
2. You must have a compelling reason why habit change is necessary for you. What aspect of the change makes you excited to try it out?
3. Develop your plan for success.
4. Make the path ahead easy, with the least amount

of resistance possible for yourself.

5. You must introduce a cue or reminder to complete the habit, such as a to-do checklist.

To help you out, here is an example of how the implementation phase might go. It is a three-step process made firstly by identifying the goal, establishing a reason why it matters, and then creating a plan to implement the change that will bring you to your goal.

- *Identification Stage*: I have identified that I need to drink 2,000 mL (approx. 4 – 5 large glasses) of fresh water per day and eliminate my soft drink consumption in the process.

- *My Why*: I know that soft drinks are very high in sugar and provide no health benefits, only empty calories. They can contribute to poor oral health and weight gain.

- *Three Day Implementation Plan*: Drink 500 mL of fresh water each day and reduce my soft drink consumption to no more than 330 mL (1 can of soft-drink) per day.

You will note that the three-day implementation plan does not yet meet the goal identified in the example. It is only a starting point you can continue to expand upon until your goal is being met or even exceeded. Now that you have your basic idea, you can begin to take action to implement it in your life. Again, start small and build your actions in tiny steps.

1. Plan on a Sunday

This is more personal preference than a hard and fast rule, but I find that it helps to make my plans on a Sunday. I like to start my week on Monday with the plans fresh in my mind, ready to make a change for the new week. Additionally, since Sunday is my rest day from physical activity, I have more time to plan and make adjustments if they are needed. If you have had little luck implementing plans before, I would suggest giving this a try.

2. Write up your 72-hour "Switch Plan."

Your Switch Plan should involve pinpointing two specific habits. First, isolate just one habit that you know will improve your overall health in the long term. Try to make your choice very specific and achievable. For example, take the previous scenario, where the positive habit is drinking 500 mL per water a day as a target. Next, identify a diet habit that you know has been detrimental to your health, preferably one that is related to the positive habit you want to introduce. Choose something that occurs relatively frequently for you. In this case, we will again use consuming soft drinks.

Now determine the incremental change that you can do over the next three days. This is not a lot of time, so think small. You may not be able to cut out soft drink entirely during this time, but you can probably cut it back to 330 mL a day if you tried. Likewise, you may not hit 2,000 mL of water in the first three days, but you could try to drink 500 mL or just three cups. You are trying to gradually reduce the bad habit by gradually increasing the good habit.

3.   Make it easy

For the most part, your goals themselves are going to be easy. This is part of keeping them sustainable. The most challenging part is not doing the action itself, but remembering to do it and keeping up with it throughout the day. Drinking water is not hard, but it can slip your mind easily. To remedy this issue, find ways to remind yourself of your goals periodically. Here are a few sample methods for keeping drinking enough water at the forefront of your mind.

If you are trying to drink 500 mL of water, purchase and use a 500 mL water bottle. This way, you know exactly what that much water looks like and how close you are to completing your goal at any given time. You can easily track your progress just by looking at your water bottle. In time, you can build up to a larger 2L bottle, but for now, focus on the 72-hour goal. Also, try to resist the temptation of drinking the whole bottle in one go and getting it out of the way. We are trying to build a habit that eventually gets expanded to 2,000 mL, and it would be highly unusual to drink that much water at once and on a regular basis. Splitting up your hydration throughout the day encourages you to build the habit following the same schedule, so stick to 100-150 mL each time you drink and quench your thirst over a longer period. This will have the added benefit of reducing the urge for other drinks later in the day, as you still have water to drink.

This one may be obvious, but it is often overlooked. Keep the bottle nearby and place it somewhere you look at frequently throughout the day. Keeping it in your line of sight and easily accessible makes it easier to return to it throughout the day. This might mean keeping it on your office desk or taking it with you to place in the cupholder in your car. The added visual cue may be enough for you to take frequent sips throughout the day, but if not, set the alarm on your phone to go off in two-hour intervals reminding you to drink. Some water bottles even come equipped with built-in timers that flash to remind you to drink. These timers become a cue that "triggers your brain to initiate a behavior. It is a bit of information that predicts a reward" (Clear, n.d.-b, para. 11), in this case, better hydration. Think of it like conditioning yourself to anticipate drinking water and automate the process. Daily habits are best ingrained into our lives when we do an action frequently and not just every few days or once or twice a week, so be sure to stick to the timers you have set for the remainder of the 72 hours.

Practical Step 2

Increase the frequency

The 72-hour trial run is meant to ease you into a new habit. Now you can begin to increase the frequency that you perform the habit. Reflect on how the last three days went. Is there anything you need to tweak? Is the cue you have chosen to prompt the habit strong enough? Did you stick to the mini habits? Was it too hard, or too easy? Make any adjustments you need before proceeding. We are aiming to automate this behavior, so the more you perform it, and the more structured your behaviors are the greater success you will have in maintaining the habit.

At this point, you can use the *STOP>REVIEW>PIVOT* and *POWER* method to ensure the habit you have chosen is right for you and your incremental introduction is starting to make changes. Once you have reviewed, gradually increase the length of time you do the habit and the frequency of the habit each day. For example, if you now find it easy to drink 500 mL of water a day, you can move up to a 750 mL water bottle and aim to finish it daily for the next 14 days.

Don't try to push too hard too fast; just focus on slow, incremental steps.

Practical Step 3

Structure

Give yourself the structure you need to succeed. I have personally found that if I write down the habit, I want to complete in my schedule and give myself the opportunity and motivation to do it during the day, I am about 80% more likely not just to do the habit but automate it. Grab a piece of paper and write your new habit down along with others as you introduce them. The physical process of writing down your goals is compelling, as it is a proven method for significantly multiplying your chances of success.

Let's look at a few examples of what giving your habits structure would look like.

Introduction of Habit #1: Writing down my top three priorities and key actions for the following day

Reason: Introducing this habit would allow me to have clarity and focus on my most important tasks for the next day. I could go to bed confident in the progress I will make tomorrow, and I will allow my subconscious to arrange the next day while I sleep. I then have confidence that I can wake up ready to tackle my most important tasks.

Incremental Change: I started by setting the alarm at 5:30 PM. Even if I hadn't finished my other work by then, I stopped and grabbed my notepad to write down just my number one priority for the next day. I did this for three days, after which I reviewed and increased this to two priorities for seven days. Again, I reviewed and then increased to three key tasks. I always listed my number one priority at the top and used tick boxes to mark my progress to build confidence.

Long-term Results: From just this one successfully implemented habit, I found that I had much more clarity going into the next day. I was more relaxed at night, and my focus was crystal clear. Due to its success, I decided to create *The Daily Goal Tracker* resource that lets you track over 1,000 actions each year.

I found amazing success through a simple habit I could accomplish in just a few minutes of my time every day. When I expanded the initial single priority into two and then three priorities, my successes increased exponentially. Now take a look at this second example based around improving your diet.

Introduction of Habit #2: Eat fresh salmon twice per week.

Reason: Salmon is an incredible source of nutrients for your diet. It is a powerhouse food source that provides several impressive health benefits. The Omega-3 fatty acids alone have been linked to "decreasing inflammation, lowering blood pressure, reducing the risk of cancer and improving the function of the cells that line your arteries" (Spritzler, 2016, para. 8). It is also full of B vitamins, potassium, and antioxidants.

Incremental Change: Fresh salmon inherently requires you to eat it before it goes bad, which is why I prefer fresh to frozen, which can sit in the freezer for weeks or months and does not help you form a habit. Instead, buy fresh salmon and place it so it is directly in your line of sight every time you open the fridge, such as right on the top shelf. Start with about four weeks of having one serving of salmon over a week, review, and then increase the amount to two fillets a week.

Important Note: I am very aware of the high cost of salmon. Many people will say they cannot afford to purchase fresh salmon. But when all the benefits are considered, salmon is definitely worth the price tag. In fact, I would argue that you actually cannot afford not to eat it!

Practical Step 4
Be proud at the check-out!

When I go to the grocery store, I find it intriguing to look at what others are buying. What you place on the check-out counter is a direct reflection of your diet and the energy levels you will have for the week. If you make healthy choices, you will be proud to put your food selection on display.

Recently, as I was checking out at the grocery store, I noticed the purchases of a gentleman to my left in his late 50's. I took a peek and noticed he had laid out:

1. A large bag with 24 Chinese dumplings
2. Two large chocolate blocks, 500g each
3. A small bag with eight frozen fish cakes
4. A pack of four cinnamon donuts
5. Two bottles of cola
6. Pasta sauce

7.   Two loaves of white bread

At even just a quick glance, you can tell this is not a healthy or sustainable diet. It may be a cheap and easy one, but when you start to make healthy purchases, you will feel the difference when you layout purchases you can be proud of. It is also a great way to review what you eat in a typical week.

When you next head to the store, really take notice of the carts of those around you. Would you be proud to load up with processed and heavily packaged foods, or would you be happier knowing you have made the right choice for yourself? Your goal should be at least 50% of your cart being foods that are not prepackaged. These foods are generally unhealthy and often come packed with preservatives. They are more for the temporary enjoyment your brain gets from eating something sweet or salty, but ultimately unhealthy for your body's long-term benefit.

You should feel good about what you are eating. If your guilty pleasure foods really make you feel guilty, consider why that is and if it is time to say goodbye to these guilty snacks. Make it a personal game to try to impress the people at the check-out and behind you in the line, and you will find it much easier to pick up fresh ingredients.

Practical Step 5
Organization and Application

Maintaining a healthy diet takes discipline and commitment. Your initial excitement and motivation may fade away over time when you get cravings for things you have left behind. Having the personal courage to continue making smart diet decisions, supported by good organization and planning, will keep you going. Having a clear goal and knowing the reason why you are doing all of this will help bolster your self-discipline. To accurately organize your healthy habits and apply them, you must take the proper steps to support your personal commitment.

This final practical step is inspired by the old-fashioned food pyramid that we may all have seen when you were a child. You will likely remember posters of this pyramid, maybe back in your grade school days, that provides a visual representation of what you should be eating and in what relative amounts. If you find that you sometimes slip into bad eating habits due to temptation in the fridge or pantry, try this instead.

Use your fridge and pantry to create a sort of visual food pyramid of your own, dividing up what you need to eat most and least of. The top shelf, the most readily available to your eye line when you open the fridge, should contain what you should eat most of. This includes foods like salmon, fresh vegetables, fruit, and other dietary staples. In the pantry, this means whole grains. The middle shelf contains things you eat only occasionally, like nonfat Greek yogurt, eggs, and low-fat cheese. The bottom shelf is restricted to just a couple of small treats. Once these are gone, that is all for the week. It may also help if you label your shelving by creating stickers. Whatever allows you to create a sound system is worth making it obvious.

Self-control is critical, and this system makes it easier than ever to not be tempted by opening the fridge and immediately seeing the rare treats rather than the staple foods. Your goal then should be to eat everything on your top shelf.

Chapter 5

How to Switch on Your Fitness and Exercise Habits

You do not need to become a dedicated super athlete to have a healthy exercise routine. Your goal should be to do a little bit of exercise every day to ensure you remain active and develop positive fitness habits. Not exercising can cause health impacts from weight gain to weakening muscles, bones (osteoporosis) and loss of elasticity of tendons & ligaments but as long as you stay active, you can reduce the risk of muscle atrophy (degeneration of muscle) and keep your strength up as you age. On top of direct physical benefits, exercise can have significant mental benefits as well. It can help you feel more energetic, refreshed and less stressed. With all these benefits, finding a little time to work out throughout the day is a no-brainer. Consistency is more important than how strenuous the workout is, so pick exercises that don't put too much strain on you and fit well into your typical schedule and lifestyle.

They Have It All Wrong! - Why Pain Doesn't Equal Gain

Fitness shouldn't be painful unless you are specifically training for an event and need to 'stretch' beyond your usual comfort zone. This doesn't mean you should never work up a sweat and be 'uncomfortable' at times, but it does mean that you don't have to risk exhaustion or injury to get healthy. Trying to push yourself too hard too fast can lead to an unsustainable workout schedule. Instead, stick to the mini habit's method. I recommend knowing your starting point, and this way you can pick the activities that are comfortable, realistic and suitable for you, and build slowly at a pace that feels right. If you don't think you could jog for 20 minutes, start with just five minutes and build your way up to longer jogs. It is admirable to decide you want to improve your fitness for any reason be it for an event, a health scare or increasing weight. I therefore want you to start slowly, build a solid base and progress with a sensible and long-term approach. I see too many people that try to hit the ground running, rather than starting at a slow walk and getting faster over time. This approach often can lead to giving up when lofty goals are not met. If you increase incrementally and start where you are comfortable, you are much more likely to continue the habit and enjoy the journey to your health and fitness goals.

January is a huge month for gyms, so much so that "in a 2017 survey of nearly 6,400 fitness clubs in the U.S., the International Health, Racquet & Sports club Association found that 10.8 percent of all gym membership sales in 2016 took place in January, which is proportionally more than any other month that year" (Poon, 2019, para. 6). This makes January gym memberships seem like a great idea at first, as there is a big cultural push, but fitness is not seasonal, and many of the people who boast about their new resolutions don't even make it to February. The unfortunate truth is that fewer than 10% of the January rush will maintain their gym visits after the first three months. This is in part because these sorts of resolutions are rarely well-planned. They are hardly thought about during the feasting of the winter holidays, and once the initial enthusiasm wears off, people lose interest without a solid plan. Again, if you do not know your ideal outcome and the steps to reach it, how can you tell if your efforts are making a difference? By mid-January, many people exhaust themselves, lose their motivation when they don't see immediate results, and simply give up.

Why People Give Up On Exercise

Many health institutions rightly point out that people need to change their health habits, but simply saying this and not giving people the tools and mindset they need to succeed can be a narrow-minded approach. To understand how to stick with exercise past January, we must first understand why so many people aren't willing to keep working out.

1. **They don't develop a plan**

   It is critical to know what your goals are and the frequency you expect yourself to exercise, or you cannot hold yourself accountable for these goals. More importantly, your reason for exercise needs to be compelling enough that it enables you to power through the desire to quit.

2. **They are in a rush for immediate results**

   Many people I have consulted with believe they need to hit their top speed on day one. This idea is reinforced by exposure to shows like The Biggest Loser, which has contestants dragging tractor tires on the first day and collapsing due to exhaustion, but this kind of exercise is unsustainable, and they have medical personnel on-site for a reason. This Habit Switch is about the idea of small, sustainable change with a long-term view. Under no circumstances do I want you to attempt to start a long-term activity at top speed!

3. They don't accommodate for their age and ability

As we get older, whether we want to admit it or not, our body's limitations change. As an example, I used to be able to dunk a basketball in my 20's. I went to the courts with my son recently and tried to show off, and after some warm-ups, stretching, and a few attempts, I was lucky if I could get within four inches of the hoop with my fingertips, let alone my whole wrist. Needless to say, my son wasn't too impressed with his dad!

I would love to be capable of all the things I could do in my 20's, but it is better for my fitness to accept what I can still do rather than keep trying to do things I can't anymore. As we start moving towards 30 years of age and older, our range of motion (R.O.M) decreases around our joints, and our muscles and tendons don't have the elasticity or strength they used to. These limitations are even more evident if you try to push yourself too hard. By starting slow, you give yourself so much more opportunity to strengthen muscles that have been in 'hibernation' for a few years.

As an example, here's a typical scenario for someone who fails to accommodate for their ability and jumps into exercise too quickly:

1. They notice they are gaining weight and think, "I have to do something about this, and fast!"

2. They Google local gyms or fitness camps.

3. They pay their membership fees with every intention of going for the 12 months they signed up for.

4. They get to the first session. Their energy and enthusiasm is pumping.

5. They push themselves hard on the first session for an hour. It's painful, but they see others well in advance of their current fitness and try to emulate their pace.

6. They get home, feeling exhausted but great about the session.

7. They wake up the following morning, feeling very stiff and sore. They say, "No problem, it's just a bit of muscle soreness."

8. They go to their next session. This time, motivation has dropped, the weights feel a lot heavier, and their muscles still feel sore. They push through the session, but it's only 50 minutes this time rather than the scheduled

hour.

9. During the next day, they feel even worse, sore all over from the workout. Even lifting their arm to brush their teeth becomes a chore.

10. When the next session is scheduled, something comes up at work. They think, "That's okay; I'll do it next time."

11. The session after that, they begrudgingly grab their gear, but nothing seems exciting about this anymore. They look around and see people effortlessly lifting weights, and their confidence takes a big hit.

12. They arrive home, sit on the couch, and think, "Maybe I'll take a break until my muscles are less sore."

13. Despite their best intentions, they never seem to be able to return, even after the soreness has faded.

Pushing yourself too hard is a one-way ticket to scaring yourself off the practice of exercise. It is immeasurably better to attend 20 sessions of low-activity exercise in a month than two sessions of high-activity exercise.

1. *The activity isn't sustainable*

I'm a huge advocate for activities you can keep doing into your 60's and 70's like power walking, cycling, swimming, dancing, golf, water aerobics, or other low-impact exercises. If you're in your teens, 20's, and 30's, then, by all means, participate in higher impact activities, but making sure that at least some of your exercise is sustainable for years to come is a great way to focus on the long term without increasing your risk of injury.

2. *The activity isn't enjoyable*

You should be doing activities you find fun. Lighten up a jog with music, or replace it with a dance routine. Do yoga with a group of friends. Your ability to keep exercising is dependent on you enjoying what you do.

3. *The activity is too expensive*

Some activities involve start-up costs related to equipment or ongoing costs in the form of classes or gym memberships. If you cannot afford to keep paying for the activity, you are unlikely to stick with it. Luckily, there are many cheap or free alternatives you can do if the cost is a barrier of entry for you.

4.   *They don't STOP>REVIEW>PIVOT and POWER*

Developing your plan is your number one step for success, but it is just as important to take time to review your progress. Periodically decide if anything needs to change and if you need to make adjustments, determine how they can be structured into your daily routine and then power forward.

How did I manage to achieve my goal of 1,000 sit-ups per week in less than 90 days?

1,000 sit-ups in a week sounds like a lot, but in practice, it is easier to implement than you may think. In fact, it is something I now enjoy and have integrated into my morning routine as I mentioned at the beginning of the book. I want to walk you through my own process of integrating this exercise into my daily habits so that you can see firsthand the benefits of incremental, consistent increases in the frequency that you exercise.

- *Implementation Phase Example*: Goal of 1,000 sit-ups each week
- *Identification*: I need to increase my core abdominal strength.
- *My Why*: I want to reduce the chances of lower back pain that plagued me in my mid to late '30s so I can continue to play with my children.
- *Three Day Implementation Plan*: Following my early morning walk and breakfast, I will do 10 sit-ups each day for the next three days. The long-term plan is to build up to 170 sit-ups per day, six days per week to exceed my target of 1,000 sit-ups.

Next, I needed to make the process easy for myself. I needed to establish a cue for doing this activity that would encourage me to get it done every day.

1. I had an old yoga mat I hadn't used for ages, under my bed collecting dust. I brought it into the kitchen and rolled it up and placed it next to the dishwasher. I made sure it was easily accessible so I had somewhere comfortable to do my sit-ups.

2. To ensure I had my cue, I laid the yoga mat out on the floor before I left for my walk, as I'd have to literally walk over it when I came back.

3. I arrived back from my walk, had breakfast, and then as I walked back into the kitchen with my breakfast bowl, the yoga mat was right there.

4. I then completed 10 sit-ups and repeated this pattern for three days in a row. It wasn't enough to make me feel sore, but I had effectively laid the groundwork for a solid structure and a helpful reminder of my goal.

5. At my three-day review, I then planned that each day I would increase my sit-ups incrementally by three extra each day. When I reached 20, I would then split my sit-ups into sets of 10 with a rest in between.

6. Over the next 30 days, I then slowly increased my sit-ups by two each day. On Monday mornings, I increased by five, then reverted to increments of two for the rest of the week. As I progressed, I made sure I was doing sets of 15 or 20 at a time rather than doing them all at once.

My weekly goal plan to achieve 170 Sit-ups p/day

	MON	TUES	WED	THU	FRI	SAT	Rest Day
Week 1	10	12	14	16	18	20	
Week 2	25	27	29	31	33	35	
Week 3	40	42	44	46	48	50	
Week 4	55	57	59	61	63	65	
	MON	TUES	WED	THU	FRI	SAT	Rest Day
Week 5	70	72	74	76	78	80	
Week 6	85	87	89	91	93	95	
Week 7	100	102	104	106	108	110	
Week 8	115	117	119	121	123	125	
	MON	TUES	WED	THU	FRI	SAT	Rest Day
Week 9	130	132	134	136	138	140	
Week 10	145	147	149	151	153	155	
Week 11	160	162	164	166	168	170	

As this process demonstrates, I simply started small by developing my system and making progress easy. I now do over 4,000 sit-ups a month. This equates to 48,000 per year! If I had started by trying to do 70-100 sit-ups a day, I would have been sore and risked an abdominal strain, which might have made me give up altogether. Now I am capable of doing that many without much strain because I have slowly built up to it. You will also notice I included a rest day in my schedule, which is imperative as a reward system and as also recovery and repair for my abdominals. If I want to continue to increase my sit-ups, I would give myself two rest days to compensate. You can apply the above structure to any exercise or fitness habit you want to implement into your own life.

Don't Aim for Elite Fitness

Unless you are aiming to be the next big thing in the fitness world, you don't have to train like an elite athlete. I would recommend that you don't, and you instead stick to fitness habits that suit your lifestyle and capabilities. The definition by Segen's Medical Dictionary of an elite athlete is one who is considered to be "a person who is currently or has previously competed as a varsity player (individual or team), a professional player or a national or international level player". Chances are you are just trying to get your health up, so if you are not a professional athlete, why try to mirror the exercise habits of Olympians?

Keep in mind that elite athletes are under the supervision of personal trainers and coaches that know how hard they can push. They also have access to medical aid should it be required. Trying to become elite can be dangerous with or without the right resources. This book isn't trying to help you rise to the top of your exercise field; I only want to help you establish habits that you can integrate into a 40-60 hour work week, not ones that take a full-time commitment.

Your aim should be to develop a level of fitness that best suits your goals and preferred outcomes. This means worrying about the long term too. There are very few sports that athletes are in for more than 15 years, with some even less than that. This is not sustainable, nor is it achievable on a regular schedule. Try to stick to habits that you can continue to complete for decades and whether you are working, on vacation, or even travelling for work.

The Seven Tips to Implement Your Habit Plan: How to Master a Fitness Plan for the Long Term

There are seven main tips to keep in mind so you can ensure you have all the knowledge you need to establish a fitness plan that lasts. These serve to summarize the chapter and give you simple, concise steps you can follow. If you master these tips, you will be in control of your physical health.

Healthy Fitness Step 1

Write down your five-year fitness goal

Writing down your five-year goal gives you a long-term focus rather than a short-term one. Once your five-year goal has been established, break that down into smaller steps and goals to achieve. I recommend you start each habit with the three-day trial run.

Setting fitness goals is a fantastic way to remain motivated. Your short-term fitness goals provide you with a close, relatively easy target to focus on, and you build your self-confidence while in the process. Your long-term goals keep your overall objective in the front of your mind, pushing you to keep exercising every day. When you reach your goals, check them off on your list and make new ones so you can continue moving forward.

Healthy Fitness Step 2

Fitness should be fun, not a chore

If you love your workout, it will never feel like a chore. Pick exercises that make you legitimately excited to get active. This will help keep you from dropping your routine. You should look forward to hitting the gym, going for a power walk or taking a jog, not dread it. When you're having fun, you won't have time to worry about these fears that could otherwise hold you back.

Healthy Fitness Step 3

Be very mindful of the ongoing expense of your fitness activity

If costs get too high, they can discourage you from continuing with your plan. Equipment, memberships, transportation, and travel costs can add up and make your exercise plan unsustainable. To avoid this, determine what the upfront costs for your exercise plan are and then look at the 12-month costs to see if you could keep up with them. Try to do 30-60 day trials first to ensure you really want to pay for a product or service. I'm sure there are many people with expensive road bikes, golf clubs, exercise bikes, 12-month gym memberships, and kayaks sitting unused in a garage or closet, gathering dust. Avoid making any ultimately unnecessary purchases.

Healthy Fitness Step 4

Build your fitness slowly - your body will thank you for it!

As mentioned previously, small steps are key. Build momentum with consistent change, frequent repetition, and structure while always keeping long-term benefits in mind. If you choose to go 0-100 right out of the gate, you risk early burnout, lethargy, despondency, injury, and other potential health consequences.

Healthy Fitness Step 5

Fuel your body with the right foods to maintain energy

You may have every intention of developing a solid fitness plan and exercise habits, but if you don't have the diet to back it up, it will fall through. You need to ensure you are getting enough fuel and the right kind of energy for your workouts. Many people are willing to feed their car with premium gasoline to get better performance, but they do not realize that the same rule applies to their own body in the form of their diet. Give yourself the premium fuel you need to succeed.

Healthy Fitness Step 6

Have a Fitness Accountability Partner

Your Fitness Accountability Partner is someone who helps ensure you are staying on track. This person or group can be a friend, spouse, colleague, coach, or anyone that will encourage you to reach your goals. This system works particularly well when you have a training partner to keep you accountable for your exercise. In this circumstance, they may also need your support and aid when they are struggling through rough stages themselves. Lean on each other and share the experience of lifelong fitness as you exercise together.

Healthy Fitness Step 7

Be organized and create the least resistance

When implementing habits for exercise and diet, some habits may be more difficult than others. Make them as easy as possible to adopt by creating the lowest resistance to starting. Keep your habits small until you know you can do them. You may want to arrange things the night prior to starting a habit, so you have fewer reasons not to do it the next day. It also means having a specific time set for exercise. Structure will aid you immensely.

My personal example for my morning walks:

1. Before going to bed each night, I get my exercise gear ready. This way, I'm not fumbling around in the dark to get what I need.
2. I pre-set my podcast so I can just hit play.
3. The dog leash is ready at the back door.

By getting all of this done the night before, getting ready to exercise only involves getting out of bed and getting dressed.

For additional motivation, check out the Canadian Medical Association Journal study "Health Benefits of Physical Activity: The Evidence." It contains a breakdown of the benefits of exercise, which include a direct relationship with reducing cardiovascular disease and a wide variety of other conditions, including diabetes mellitus; cancer, namely colon and breast cancer; obesity; hypertension; bone and joint diseases like osteoporosis and osteoarthritis; and depression.

Chapter 6

Avoiding a Habit

Short-Circuit

A habit short circuit occurs when you are unable to keep pace with the habits you have established for yourself. You begin to slip behind, taking days off that turn into weeks and then months, all while promising you will get back to work soon but having no real intention of doing so. When troubles arise, such as old bad habits rearing their heads, you need to know how to efficiently tackle them and get back into the swing of things. You also need to know how to keep this habit short circuit from happening in the first place. This involves sticking to incremental change rather than large leaps, accepting your own limitations, working with others to achieve your goal, and most importantly knowing your motivation. I will break down these methods for dodging habit short circuits below.

When Bad Habits Re-Emerge

You are very likely to slip back into a bad habit or two at some point. What may start as a single instance of breaking your diet or fitness routine can quickly spiral out of hand. If you don't have a strong enough reason behind your desire for change, you may not be able to resist these bad habits when they appear. If you feel strongly about kicking the poor habits, you can start to understand why this relapse occurs so you can prevent it next time. Ask yourself, "Was there any particular event or feeling you had that triggered this change of mindset? Was there a particular event in your life that caused a change in structure?" Understanding the real cause of returning to negative habits can shed light on the common triggers preceding each instance of relapse. Identifying these triggers helps you become more aware of your weak points. So, how can you get back on track?

Revisit Your Schedule

Your weak point may be in your schedule. If you cannot reliably stick to your schedule, either because it is too packed or too loose, you will start to make excuses for not following it. My morning habits are heavily disciplined, which means I know I can get all of my morning habits done on time. Adopting a schedule with a similar level of structure can help ensure you don't procrastinate on your goals. Rework your schedule until it fits your life.

Use Existing Momentum

Use the success and momentum you have built up with other habits to get those that have slipped back on track. Don't waste time doing the habit equivalent of staring at a blank page, waiting for words to come. Start working on adjacent goals and use the progress you make on those to revisit the habits that stumped you. Succeeding at integrating a habit boosts your self-confidence, which gives you the burst of positivity you need to tackle tougher habits.

Don't Miss More Than Two Days

Taking long breaks between your habits can cause them to fade out of your body's memory. Staying consistent is especially important during the early phases of building a habit, as taking breaks longer than 48 hours can start to weaken the links that turn habits into an automatic process. If you need to rest, it is better to take two non-consecutive days off.

Make Your Environment Conducive to Success

Environmental factors can play an important role in either keeping your motivated or aiding distraction and the return of bad habits. If you still have a cabinet full of high fat and high sugar foods, you will be tempted to break your healthy eating habits every time you open the pantry. If you keep the TV on while you work, you may spend more time watching it than getting anything done. I like getting up early to read and exercise as it is such a quiet and peaceful time with relatively few distractions. Figure out what your ideal environment is and take steps to make your surroundings match.

Your environment does not just mean physical space. It also refers to the music and media you listen to that can impact your energy levels, as well as the people you surround yourself with. If those close to you are frequently encouraging you to make bad choices, preventing you from keeping your habits or even forcing you to change something you do not feel similarly passionate about changing, you may need to reevaluate who you spend time with. Fill your life with people and things that support your goals, and you will find it much easier to keep your good habits around.

Mix Things Up

Try things out and see what works, and if one thing doesn't work, swap it for something else. Make improving your fitness an adventure and use it as an excuse to try new things. Above all else, don't constrain yourself to my schedule or anyone else's. What works for me or anyone else may not necessarily fit your schedule, lifestyle, or environment. Never try to conform to the schedule and habits of someone else if it does not positively impact you to do so. Try different schedules and routines until, and you find the one that works for you.

Revisit Your Goals to Ensure Alignment

The more time you spend writing down, reading, and reviewing your goals, the more they are programmed into your subconscious. Make sure your goals still align with what you want in life one month, six months, five years, and even ten years after setting them. Some recommend doing this review process every morning during what is called the "Golden Hour," or the first hour you are awake. This is the perfect time to revisit your goals because "the things that you do in the first hour prepare your mind and set you up for the entire day. During the first thirty to sixty minutes, take time to think and review your plans for the future" (Tracy, n.d.-b, para. 3). Getting a good start and reiterating the importance of your goals makes those goals stand out more as you go about the rest of the day.

The Resilience Factor

Resiliency can help you bounce back after even the toughest of stumbling blocks. Each time you forge ahead after a setback, you improve your resilience. The decision to keep going will help you continue to build positive habits even when they become hard to maintain. Change can be difficult, so don't expect everything to be smooth sailing. The question is not whether you will struggle or pass with flying colors; the question is whether or not you will pick yourself up, dust yourself off, and keep moving after a setback occurs.

Reward and Celebration – The Goal Loop

One area I have yet to discuss is the celebration after a victory. When you have achieved success, small or large, take time to celebrate it. Little rewards can boost your morale and encourage you to keep moving.

To enable my clients to have a visual of what this celebration looks like, I designed the 'GOAL LOOP' system as outlined in my book Magnetic Goals.

Below is an excerpt from this book to highlight the importance of celebration.

The Purpose of the Goal Loop

The goal loop provides a concrete, cyclical structure for all of your goal progress. It operates on the principles of rhythm, repetition, structure, clarity, and action. The phases allow you to develop a familiar rhythm of goal setting and achieving with positive feedback in the form of celebrating at the end. Because the phases loop back on themselves, they use repetition to encourage you to complete future goals. This process is similar to the repetition involved in daily habits which cause them to feel second nature after you have had enough practice incorporating them into your life. The goal loop is structured with an easy to follow path, so you always know what the next step is, and there is no opportunity to waste precious time. It provides you with clarity on your next move and how to achieve what you have always wanted. Most important of all, it encourages perpetual action rather than stagnation. Once one goal is accomplished, it is time to move onto the next. If you keep moving, there is nothing you cannot achieve. The beauty of The Goal Loop is that each time you complete the cycle, your goal setting structure and systems gain strength and become extremely robust.

Cyclical Phases

The goal loop is broken up into four phases, each of which reflects a previously discussed aspect of the goal setting and achieving process.

Phase One is establishing your goals. Use this time to understand what you want to accomplish. *Phase Two* is the development of supportive daily habits that will help you get where you want to go. In *Phase Three*, you will take daily actions that propel you towards success. These phases culminate in achieving your goals, celebrating, and starting the goal loop anew armed with the knowledge you have learned from your last cycle.

Phase One: Setting Your Goals

Goal setting is the foundation of every cycle of goal achievement. Each time you return to the goal-setting phase, consider what you have learned from the last cycle. What goals worked for you? Which ones were easy to stick to, and which ones did you have a harder time finding the right motivation for? Are the goals you are setting in this cycle, helping you to reach your 12-month goals, or have your 12-month goals changed? You should also be re-examining your *why factor* in this phase and making sure you still feel dedicated to the goals you set. Coming up with a powerful, solid set of goals that you feel passionately about in Phase One lays the foundation for the next phases and paves the way for future successes.

Phase Two: Establishing Supportive Daily Habits

You already know the amazing benefits that the right habits can have on your ability to achieve your goals. Knowing what works for you and what doesn't can help you revise and review your list of habits and identify which habits you can continue including in your schedule and which need to change. Update any habits that are specific to goals that have already been achieved to reflect your new ones. For example, if you have accomplished your first goal of weight loss and your new goal is developing muscle tone, you may need to establish a new workout routine to achieve different results. When reviewing your already existing daily habits and creating new ones, ask yourself the following questions. How is this habit helping me to achieve my current goals? Is there any new information I should direct my focus on learning? What habits were hardest to stick to last time, and why? How can I either modify these habits to make them more suited to my lifestyle and enjoyable? Answering these questions can help you keep your daily habits aligned as closely as possible to your goals.

Phase Three: Daily Action

Phase Three is about acting on the goals you have set and the habits you have chosen and taking actions every day that move you closer to the finish line. Many of the actions you take for various goals may be the same with only slight differences. For example, whether you are looking to start a new business or write a book, you will need to do research; however, the type of research you will have to do to launch your business successfully is different from the information you will have to gather for your book. You can use the actions you have completed for past goals to form a blueprint for your current ones and make the appropriate modifications when necessary. Remember to start with small actions and build up to larger ones, but keep moving forward no matter what. Daily actions help you build momentum that will carry you through to current and future goals.

Phase Four: Achieving Your Goals and Celebrating

You've done it! You have remained committed and focused, and in exchange, you have done what you have set out to do. Completing your goals can help you to feel more fulfilled on top of the benefits they already provide. The gratification from knowing your time and energy has paid off is immense. Take some time to appreciate all the hard work you have put into your success. Do something to celebrate, as you should be proud of yourself. Just ensure that it is nothing that will tip you back into performing any negative habits that you have worked so hard to eradicate.

Next, it is time to roll all of these positive feelings into motivation to tackle your next goal. You are likely riding high on positive emotions, and by now, you have realized the extent of what you are capable of. Success is a very powerful motivator. Armed with the knowledge and the proof that when you truly apply yourself, you really can accomplish what once felt like a faraway dream, starting on your next dream is the natural next step. Turn this success into achieving another goal, and another, until you are working your way up to your big 3-year and 5-year goals. You already have the tools and experience to ensure you are successful; you just need to put them to use by returning to the goal-setting loop.

Decision Making with the Future in Mind

Following the path of The Goal Loop encourages you to think about your upcoming goals and your ideal future. It is a tool you can use to develop a plan that works for you and is unique to what you want to achieve while still being versatile enough to accommodate all of your goals. This means the decisions you make must also be forward-thinking as you consider what impact your choices have on your future.

Start establishing the goals you want to achieve as early as possible, so you have every possible opportunity to develop positive habits and guide your decisions in the areas you choose to focus on. If you understand the relationship between your choices, the goal loop, and the end result of your life, you can use critical turning point moments and crucial decisions to effectively alter your future.

Eradicate the Perfection Mindset

Trying to achieve perfection can be a detriment to your success. Perfect, by definition, means "complete and correct in every way, of the best possible type or without fault" (Cambridge Dictionary, n.d., para. 1). Placing the lofty expectations of being "without fault" on yourself only ensures that when you do inevitably have difficulties, as you are only human, you will be much harder on yourself than you would if you kept realistic expectations. If you "allow yourself to do things incompletely, imperfectly, and imprecisely," you will "progress to the state of completion and precision" (Chua, n.d., para. 13) rather than getting bogged down in ensuring everything is perfect. It is better to get two 90% grades than one 100% and one 0% because you weren't able to move on from the first assignment. You may even be able to use your experience completing both tasks to get better at future ones.

Of course, if social media posts are to be believed, perfect people are everywhere. However, these posts are entirely curated to suggest this; you don't see the hundreds of failed attempts, only a single success. Additionally, not everyone's idea of perfection will align, making it even more of an impossible goal. Don't let yourself be deceived by these unachievable ideals.

Escaping perfectionism

Perfectionism can create additional hurdles that keep you standing still. You may never feel like you are finished with a task, or you may constantly feel stressed about your performance. You aren't able to build your skills incrementally because you are so fixated on getting to 100% as fast as possible. It can also impact your ability to try new things. If you constantly fear failure "you often adopt a mindset of, *If I can't do it perfectly, then I won't even try* [...] In essence, your fear of failure actually makes you fail" (Lombardo, 2017, para. 6). Improving your overall health is often dependent on your ability to try something new and take a risk that just might pay off.

If you are a perfectionist, how do you let go of the need to always be perfect? For one, get comfortable with the idea of failure. If you accept failure as a natural part of an attempt rather than a forbidden outcome, you will be more inclined to put yourself out there. For another, start valuing your own goals, decisions, and successes whenever they occur. Many perfectionists are overly reliant on what others think of them. Once you learn to start caring more about your own opinion of yourself and valuing your input, your need to be perfect will begin to fade. Remember that when it comes to decision making in your own life, you are the authority on yourself, and therefore you do not need to be reliant on others to decide what is right for you (Cohen, 2018, para. 15). Self-confidence will help you minimize fears of failure and bolster your self-reliance.

Group Energy - The Power of Others

If you have difficulty staying committed when you're flying solo, try joining a group of likeminded people or making one yourself. This might mean joining a sports team, working out with friends, making a swimming squad, or joining an online group that allows you to share similar experiences and questions. Knowing that others are experiencing the same things you are and sharing tips and tricks will encourage you to keep going.

Group workouts are growing increasingly popular. A 2017 study suggests that when we exercise alongside our peers, we are more likely to attend class, put in the necessary effort, and even improve our mental state. Participants who attended at least one class a week saw "a statistically significant decrease in stress, and an improvement in the mental, physical, and emotional quality of life" (Knight, 2017, para. 15).

If you want to enjoy every benefit fitness has to offer, group exercise is the way to go.

Group energy isn't just restricted to exercise. It can also help with dieting, as "one study found that 95 percent of those who started a weight-loss program with friends completed the program, compared to a 76 percent completion rate for those who tackled the program alone" (Steinhilber, 2017, para. 9). If you have others to lean on, you will find yourself more committed to hitting your goals and sticking to your habits. This is the power of support from a group.

Link It Back to Your Two Why's

All outcomes we achieve ultimately come back to two things. The first is the decisions we make, and the second is the actions we take. When you make a choice or take action, you may ask yourself, "Why did I make that decision? What is the underlying reason?" A strong desire can positively influence your decisions, while uncertainty in your goals will make good decisions harder to make.

If you find that you are regularly slipping back into bad habits, you need to determine your two 'why's. The first 'why' is why you make the choices you do, as well as how they are either positively or negatively impacting you. What is the driving motivation behind your decisions, and if it is a negative factor, what should you do to make it a positive force? The second 'why' is why you need to implement a given change. How will the change impact your long-term health?

If you are having trouble understanding your motivations, I highly recommend the "Why?" section of Luke Bremner's article "The Importance Of Understanding The 'Why' Behind Your Goals." Being in tune with and in control of your motivations will let you move forward and avoid the habit short circuit.

Chapter 7

Implement
and
Take Action

You have all the knowledge you will need to achieve success. You understand the theory behind mini habits and the amazing effect they can have on your life, as well as how to put them into practice. The only thing left for you to do is take the necessary steps to implement what you have read into your own life. Reading and collecting knowledge is great, but if you never put that knowledge into practice, you will never be able to see any change. You might read every book on basketball in the world, but if you never attempt to a 3 pointer you can hardly call yourself a basketball master.

Many people make the mistake of simply learning

and not doing. They assure themselves they will start, soon, but as the weeks and months go on, they lose the initial burst of motivation they had when they finished listening to a podcast episode or reading a book. By the time they get around to starting, they have forgotten everything they have read. The only way around this is by taking action and getting in practice as soon as possible. Starting to apply what you have read will reinforce what you've learned. You need to shift from being a huge consumer of books, audio and seminars and begin to pause and take action on those things that resonated with you, otherwise, you're much more likely to forget 90% of the material. There is no better time to start putting what you read and listen to into practice than right now.

If you find some aspect of the habit switch process slips your memory, review it as often as you need. Take notes and highlight what speaks to you. Discussing the ideas in the book with friends can help keep them fresh, and you may even convert them into a partner on your quest for better health. Involving friends can also help you get a better angle on what you have read. If you have a friend who tends to tackle problems in a different way, discussing your new plan as outlined in *The Habit Switch* with them can provide you with a new point of view and additional insights on what you have read. You may end up seeing an idea in a whole new light.

You are ready to begin the journey to a healthier, happier life. All it takes is employing the strategies you have already learned. If you can take action, you should; that is, if you feel you can make a change or implement something, then do it now. Hold yourself accountable for getting started as soon as you can. You cannot put your health on the backburner.

Actionable Items

If you are committed to getting moving right away, here are some specific, actionable items you can do right now to get started. They will make the transition from learning to doing easier and supply you with a roadmap for success.

Highlight what matters

What sections stood out to you most? Which really gave you that extra push of motivation, or provided a suggestion you would like to implement? Return to these sections and highlight the lines that really matter to you. When you return to the book in the future, you can easily find the ideas that sparked your passion and drive without necessarily needing to reread every sentence. In may only take you 10 minutes, but these reflection points will be highly valuable for you in the years to come.

Write out your goals

Figure out what goals matter most to you and start writing them down. Start with the big-ticket items, and then consider the smaller day-to-day goals you want to achieve. What habits would you need to adopt to reach your goals? What implementation strategy works best for achieving these outcomes? Once you have written out your goals, you should have a real plan you can follow.

Introduce your first goal

Start small! It is the key message of this book and the one thing I hope you keep in mind when putting my strategies into practice. Small changes lead to a big impact. Choose just one goal and give it the three-day test run. Decide what you like and what isn't working for you, rework, and try again. Don't try to introduce additional goals and habits for achieving them until you feel like you have fully integrated the first habit into your schedule. This will prevent you from overburdening yourself and give the new habit time to work its magic so you can take notice of its results.

Keep building

Increase the frequency and, slowly, the number of your habits until you are creeping closer to your goals. Continue to build off past successes and keep moving. If you stick with it and keep up your habits for health, you really can achieve a healthier body and mind.

Conclusion

Your fitness determines so many other aspects of your future. If you don't keep your body in good shape, you will not be able to experience so much of what life has to offer. Health issues resulting from poor fitness habits limit your ability to live up to your full potential. You may miss out on opportunities, be unable to perform certain tasks, or experience increased stress and other mental health woes. Your body is the vehicle by which you make your way through life, and you deserve a body that is as reliable as you need it to be.

When you prioritize your health, you unlock so many pathways that might have otherwise been barred to you. Healthy eating gives you energy, helps you manage your weight, and ensures that your body will function at full capacity. Healthy exercise builds up your strength, helps discourage weight gain, and keeps you fit long into your life. You can ensure huge future success just by taking small steps today. If you set up the right habits now, they will stay with you for 20, 30, and even 50 years down the line. Set the precedent for good health habits early and save yourself trouble in the long run.

The Power of Small

Every choice you make has an impact. Simple incremental changes and positive decisions build-up to a landslide effect. Actions that seem small in isolation, like taking a power walk through the park or drinking the daily recommended dose of water, are not so small when added up over years and years of good habits. A handful of pushups in the morning turns into hundreds, which turns into thousands, which turns into tens of thousands. If you convert an action into a habit by repeating it frequently and giving it time to grow, you will reap immense rewards.

Remember to always keep your long-term goals in mind. You won't see a change right away, but if you stick with the mini habits, you will need no help seeing the difference five years later. The difference that properly implemented mini habits can have on your life is enormous. If you need some help seeing this change early on, the STOP>REVIEW>PIVOT and POWER system is your friend.

Using Review to Your Advantage

Self-awareness is an extremely important skill for improving your health. With it, you can accurately determine which aspects of your plan are helping you and which ones aren't doing as much good as you had hoped. An honest review and acceptance of where you are, without guilt, can save you months of plugging away at an ineffective strategy.

This is where the *STOP>REVIEW>PIVOT* and *POWER* system comes into play. Use it to get a general grasp on how far you've come and where you need to go next. First, stop and take note of what you are currently doing. Then see if it is helping you achieve your specific goals. If not, pivot and adjust your habits. Finally, power on through with renewed confidence that what you are doing will get you closer to the outcome you want. With this system, you ensure that every step you take is one in the right direction. This allows you to make a positive change every single day.

Making Progress Every Day

True fitness is not about a sudden burst of activity or weight loss bookended by periods of lethargy. It is about establishing sustainable habits that set you up for long-term success. Habits ensure that you never go a day without making some kind of progress, big or small - and of course, even small progress is success unfolding at a sustainable rate. Picture your habits like a school of fish. One fish alone is not much to look at, but start multiplying that fish to hundreds, maybe even thousands more, and suddenly you have one very big school. Completing your daily habits is like adding another fish to the school, knowing that given enough time you will have something really notable on your hands.

Goal achievement and daily habits are intricately linked. You cannot have one without the other. Trying to establish habits without knowing what they are for or why you even want to bother pursuing them will leave you headed in multiple different directions at once, never really narrowing your focus or expanding upon your habits in a positive way. You need goals to serve as the coordinates for your destination. Trying to reach your goals without habits is an equally impossible task. You cannot lose weight by exercising in the gym but then rewarding yourself with a bowl of confectionery or ice-cream at home. Your habits have to support what you want to achieve. You also cannot achieve your goals overnight, and you cannot expect anything done quickly to be sustainable; you need to build up habits so that they stick with you for years. You need to be committed for the long term and never expect short term gains. To be honest, the reward for some changes can take from 6 – 12 months just to see very small results. If you can successfully do this, which I firmly believe you can, you will make continual progress towards your goals and achieve outstanding results.

Input equals output

You need to look after your body. It is absolutely imperative for all other paths to success. Even if you do not do a lot of physical work now, you will find that as you get older, there will come a time where you will notice just how long it has been since you properly stretched your muscles and joints, which can make starting an exercise and weight loss plan much harder execute. You would not allow a boat to sit at port for months or years, completely without maintenance, and then try to take it out on the sea in the middle of a storm and expect to have a successful voyage. Treat your body with the same consideration. The maintenance and prep work you give to your body in the form of diet and exercise will keep you in top condition so you can be prepared for even the roughest of storms.

Health does not have to be a painful process, nor does it have to be an amazing sudden change. If you commit yourself to your habits every day, you can flip the habit switch on and jumpstart your progress towards attaining a healthy body and living a more fulfilling, healthy, and happy life.

To conclude, I wanted to leave you with this from the legendary Les Brown, US motivational speaker and author. I think he sums your potential up perfectly with this quote.

"I know something about you, even not knowing you, that you have greatness within you. You have the ability to do things that you can't even begin to imagine. You have talents and skills in you that you haven't even begun to reach for yet. When you are working at your dreams, people say, the harder the battle, the sweeter the victory. It's good because when the battle is hard, and you struggle, it's what you become in the process that is more important. It's the kind of person you become, the character that you build, the courage that you develop, the faith that you manifest. It's great when you wake up in the morning, and you look yourself in the mirror, and you're a different kind of person. You walk with a different kind of spirit. It doesn't matter what happens to you; what matters is what you are going to do about it! Easy is not an option."

I know you can do this because you are now equipped with the knowledge, the steps and the systems to make a significant change in your life. It's time to turn on **The Habit Switch**!

PLEASE LEAVE A REVIEW

I would greatly appreciate if you enjoyed this bundle book to leave a review.

You may also be interested in joining the EXCLUSIVE Review Team to receive future books in return for leaving an honest review.

To be part of the **Exclusive Book Review** Team, please visit www.thelifegraduate.com and go to the contact tab on the website.

ABOUT THE AUTHOR

Romney is the founder of The Life Graduate and author of 6 books including **The Habit Switch, Magnetic Goals, The Power of the Attraction Mindset, The Daily Goal Tracker** and **Job Launch**.

He has represented Australia in the World Championships in Dragon Boat Racing, he is a business coach, motivational speaker, qualified teacher, author and owner of two rapidly growing businesses in the educational space.

Romney has dedicated the past 20 years to helping others achieve success and fulfillment in their lives through his coaching, teaching, masterclasses, mentoring, resources and books. His clients speak of his passion and dedication for self-improvement and bringing that knowledge and experience to help others achieve what they want in their lives.

He is a sought-after speaker and is regarded as one of the leading experts in goal setting and daily habits with the development of the unique Dr. ACTION™ and 'The Goal Loop' systems. He has a Bachelor of Education in Physical Education, is a qualified Personal Trainer and has previously held Head of Faculty positions in some of the most prestigious schools in Australia. He has also held senior executive positions in leading growth companies and currently has an advisory role at Australia's largest provider of mobile dental to schools.

Please refer to the below details to reach out to Romney for speaking engagements, podcasts or other media requests.

Web. www.thelifegraduate.com

LinkedIn. Romney Nelson

The Daily Goal Tracker (Journal)
Testimonial by Brian Tracy

Resources

A.D.A.M. (2018, April 23). Facts about polyunsaturated fats. Retrieved February 16, 2020, from https://medlineplus.gov/ency/patientinstructions/000747.htm

Altrogge, S. (2019, April 30). 12 Morning and Evening Routines That Will Set Up Each Day for Success. Retrieved February 16, 2020, from https://zapier.com/blog/daily-routines/

American Academy of Family Physicians. (2017, March 27). Hydration: Why It's So Important. Retrieved February 16, 2020, from https://familydoctor.org/hydration-why-its-so-important/

American Academy of Family Physicians. (2019, July 22). Vegetarian Diet: How to Get the Nutrients You Need. Retrieved February 16, 2020, from https://familydoctor.org/vegetarian-diet-how-to-get-the-nutrients-you-need/

Barradell, S., Ennals, P., Burnett, M., Murphy, F., Karasmanis, S., & Connors, A. (2019, February 20). Reflective practice in health. Retrieved February 16, 2020, from https://latrobe.libguides.com/reflectivepractice

Beer, S. (2019, September 30). Why seasonal diets could be the answer to food sustainability. Retrieved February 16, 2020, from

https://www.independent.co.uk/news/health/seasonal-diets-food-sustainability-climate-change-crisis-a9116981.html

Better Health Channel. (2012, October). Vegetarian and vegan eating. Retrieved February 16, 2020, from https://www.betterhealth.vic.gov.au/health/healthyliving/vegetarian-and-vegan-eating

Better Health Channel. (2015, June). Physical activity – Setting yourself goals. Retrieved February 16, 2020, from https://www.betterhealth.vic.gov.au/health/healthyliving/physical-activity-setting-yourself-goals

Bjarnadottir, A. (2019, January 3). 9 Popular Weight Loss Diets Reviewed. Retrieved February 16, 2020, from https://www.healthline.com/nutrition/9-weight-loss-diets-reviewed

Breene, S. (2013, October 7). 13 Unexpected Benefits of Exercise. Retrieved February 16, 2020, from https://greatist.com/fitness/13-awesome-mental-health-benefits

Briggs, S. (2015, February 10). 25 Ways to Develop a Growth Mindset. Retrieved February 16, 2020, from https://www.opencolleges.edu.au/informed/features/develop-a-growth-mindset/

Cambridge Dictionary. (n.d.). Transformational. Retrieved February 16, 2020, from https://dictionary.cambridge.org/dictionary/english/transformational

Candelaria, K. B. (2016, April 6). Health Buzzwords: How Food Marketing Is Misleading You. Retrieved February 16, 2020, from http://www.fitnesshq.com/food-marketing/

Clear, J. (n.d.-a). How to Master the Art of Continuous Improvement. Retrieved February 16, 2020, from https://jamesclear.com/continuous-improvement

Clear, J. (n.d.-b). The 3 R's of Habit Change: How To Start New Habits That Actually Stick. Retrieved February 16, 2020, from https://jamesclear.com/three-steps-habit-change

Clear, J. (n.d.-c). Why Small Habits Make a Big Difference. Retrieved February 16, 2020, from https://fs.blog/2018/12/habits-james-clear/

Dallasnews Administrator. (2013, April 15). The dangers of salt and sugar - And how to protect yourself. Retrieved February 16, 2020, from https://www.dallasnews.com/news/healthy-living/2013/04/15/the-dangers-of-salt-and-sugar-and-how-to-protect-yourself/

Davis, L. (n.d.). Always looking forwards? It might be time to reflect. Retrieved February 16, 2020, from https://this.deakin.edu.au/self-improvement/always-looking-forwards-it-might-be-time-to-reflect

EvolutionEat. (2017, February 24). Fixed Mindset vs Growth Mindset. Retrieved February 16, 2020, from https://evolutioneat.com/fixed-mindset-vs-growth-mindset/

Foroux, D. (n.d.). The Power Of Compounding: You Can Achieve Anything, If You Stop Trying To Do Everything. Retrieved February 16, 2020, from https://dariusforoux.com/the-power-of-compounding/

Frost-Sharratt, C. (n.d.). Eating Habits Learned in Childhood are Not All Good. Retrieved February 16, 2020, from https://www.weightlossresources.co.uk/food/behaviour-eating-habits.htm

Gardner, B., Lally, P., & Wardle, J. (2012). Making health habitual: The psychology of 'habit-formation' and general practice. *British Journal of General Practice*, 62(605), 664–666. doi: 10.3399/bjgp12X659466

Gardner, B., & Rebar, A. L. (2019, January 15). Habit Formation and Behavior Change. Retrieved from https://www.oxfordbibliographies.com/view/document/obo-9780199828340/obo-9780199828340-0232.xml

Good Magazine. (n.d.). We are what we eat. Retrieved February 16, 2020, from https://good.net.nz/article/we-are-what-we-eat

Gunnars, K. (2018, July 25). Intermittent Fasting 101 - The Ultimate Beginner's Guide. Retrieved February 16, 2020, from https://www.healthline.com/nutrition/intermittent-fasting-guide

Gunnars, K. (2018, May 23). Why Is Fiber Good for You? The Crunchy Truth. Retrieved February 16, 2020, from https://www.healthline.com/nutrition/why-is-fiber-good-for-you

Hall, S. H. (2016, October 25). Why writing down your 3 MIT's at night can change your life. Retrieved February 16, 2020, from https://www.onepagecrm.com/blog/make-time-change-life/

Harvard Healthbeat. (n.d.). 7 ways to jumpstart healthy change in your life. Retrieved February 16, 2020, from https://www.health.harvard.edu/healthbeat/7-ways-to-jumpstart-healthy-change-in-your-life

Heart UK. (n.d.). Saturated fat. Retrieved February 16, 2020, from https://www.heartuk.org.uk/low-cholesterol-foods/saturated-fat

Heijligers, H. (n.d.). Don't expect results too quickly (GrowthMindset Hacks Series). Retrieved February 16, 2020, from https://smartleadershiphut.com/growth-mindset/expect-results-quickly/

Hills, A. P., Byrne, N. M., Lindstrom, R., & Hill, J. O. (2013). 'Small Changes' to Diet and Physical Activity Behaviors for Weight Management. *Obesity Facts*, 6(3), 228–238. doi:10.1159/000345030

Holland, K. (2019, January 8). Your Body Wants It — How Adopting a 'Seasonal Diet' Can Make You Healthier. Retrieved February 16, 2020, from https://www.healthline.com/health-news/adopting-a-seasonal-diet-may-help-you-lose-weight#How-seasonal-eating-works

Knight, C. (2017, November 21). Group workouts shown to improve mental & physical wellbeing. Retrieved February 16, 2020, from https://www.lesmills.com/uk/fit-planet/fitness/group-exercise-research/

Kullar, P. S. (2016, July 31). 1% a day makes you 37 times better in a year. Retrieved February 16, 2020, from https://medium.com/life-maths/life-maths-1-change-a-day-make-you-37-times-better-in-1-year-eeb66db70120

Marcin, A. (2018, December 7). Are You a Healthy Weight? Weight Ranges by Height and Sex. Retrieved February 16, 2020, from https://www.healthline.com/health/how-much-should-i-weigh#bmi

Mawer, R. (2018, July 30). The Ketogenic Diet: A Detailed Beginner's Guide to Keto. Retrieved February 16, 2020, from https://www.healthline.com/nutrition/ketogenic-diet-101

Mayo Clinic Staff. (2017, August 16). Atkins Diet: What's behind the claims? Retrieved February 16, 2020, from https://www.mayoclinic.org/healthy-lifestyle/weight-loss/in-depth/atkins-diet/art-20048485

McKenna. (2019, February 2). 8 Reasons To Commit To A Healthy Lifestyle. Retrieved February 16, 2020, from https://wedtowellness.com/8-reasons-to-commit-to-a-healthy-lifestyle/

Muttucumaru, A. (2018, March 1). Why eating what's in season is good for you - and how to eat well. Retrieved February 16, 2020, from

361

https://www.getthegloss.com/article/what-s-in-season-how-to-eat-well-all-year-round

NutritionED. (n.d.). Types of Diets. Retrieved February 16, 2020, from https://www.nutritioned.org/types-of-diets.html

Poon, L. (2019, January 16). The Rise and Fall of New Year's Fitness Resolutions, in 5 Charts. Retrieved February 16, 2020, from https://www.citylab.com/life/2019/01/do-people-keep-new-years-resolution-fitness-weight-loss-data/579388/

Sample, I. (2018, April 30). The five habits that can add more than a decade to your life. Retrieved February 16, 2020, from https://www.theguardian.com/science/2018/apr/30/the-five-habits-that-can-add-more-than-a-decade-to-your-life

Sass, C. (2019, January 24). What Is the TLC Diet, and Can It Help You Lose Weight? A Nutritionist Explains. Retrieved February 16, 2020, from https://www.health.com/weight-loss/what-is-tlc-diet

Scuderi, R. (2019, October 15). How to Invest in Yourself: 3 Valuable Ways to Change Your Life. Retrieved February 16, 2020, from https://www.lifehack.org/articles/lifestyle/3-valuable-ways-to-invest-in-yourself.html

Segal, R., & Robinson, L. (2019, June). Choosing Healthy Fats. Retrieved February 16, 2020, from https://www.helpguide.org/articles/healthy-eating/choosing-healthy-fats.htm

Segen's Medical Dictionary. (2011). Elite Athlete. Retrieved February 16, 2020, from https://medical-dictionary.thefreedictionary.com/elite-athlete

Semeco, A. (2017, February 10). The Top 10 Benefits of Regular Exercise. Retrieved February 16, 2020, from https://www.healthline.com/nutrition/10-benefits-of-exercise

Settembre, J. (2018, January 21). This is the insane amount millennials are spending on fitness. Retrieved February 16, 2020, from https://www.marketwatch.com/story/this-is-the-insane-amount-millennials-are-spending-on-fitness-2018-01-21

Spies, D. (2018, April 6). 5 Tips To Create More Self Discipline for Health Weight Loss. Retrieved February 16, 2020, from https://cleananddelicious.com/5-tips-to-create-more-self-discipline-for-health-weight-loss/

Spritzler, F. (2016, December 20). 11 Impressive Health Benefits of Salmon. Retrieved February 16, 2020, from https://www.healthline.com/nutrition/11-benefits-of-salmon

Sreenivasan, S. (2017, December 15). 5 Signs That It's Time to Change Your Life's Direction. Retrieved February 16, 2020, from https://thriveglobal.com/stories/5-signs-that-it-s-time-to-change-your-life-s-direction/

Strengthminded_Erict. (2019, February 19). Misleading Claims in Health, Fitness,

and Nutrition Advertising. Retrieved February 16, 2020, from
https://www.strengthminded.com/misleading-claims-in-health-fitness-and-nutrition-advertising/

Tracy, B. (n.d.-a). 6 Reasons Setting Goals Is Important. Retrieved February 16, 2020, from https://www.briantracy.com/blog/personal-success/importance-of-goal-setting/

Tracy, B. (n.d.-b). The Golden Hour (Continued). Retrieved February 16, 2020, from https://www.briantracy.com/blog/general/the-golden-hour-2/

Tracy, B. (n.d.-c). Turn All Your Dreams Into Reality With A Personal Development Plan. Retrieved February 16, 2020, from https://www.briantracy.com/blog/personal-success/personal-development-plan/

Tull, M. (2017, December 6). Top 10 Ways to Invest in Yourself and Why It's So Powerful. Retrieved February 16, 2020, from https://www.huffpost.com/entry/top-10-ways-to-invest-in-_b_8406130

Guidelines for a Low Cholesterol, Low Saturated Fat Diet. Retrieved February 16, 2020, from https://www.ucsfhealth.org/education/guidelines-for-a-low cholesterol-low-saturated-fat-diet

Wüest, F. (n.d.). 90% of People Quit After 3 Months of Hitting the Gym, Here's How to Be the Exception. Retrieved February 16, 2020, from https://www.lifehack.org/649556/90-of-people-quit-after-3-months-of-hitting-the-gym-heres-how-to-be-the-excep

CPSIA information can be obtained
at www.ICGtesting.com
Printed in the USA
LVHW040053121220
673919LV00001B/55